COSTA BLANCA

How to use our guide

- All the practical information, hints and tips you will need before and during the trip start on p. 100

- For general background, see the sections The Region and the People, p. 6 and A Brief History, p. 12.

- All the sights to see are listed between pp. 21 and 70. Our own choice of sights most highly recommended is pin-pointed by the Berlitz traveller symbol.

- Entertainment, nightlife and other leisure activities are described between pp. 71 and 88, while information on restaurants and cuisine is to be found on pp. 89 to 91.

- Finally, there is an index at the back of the book, pp. 126-128.

Although we make every effort to ensure the accuracy of all the information in this book, changes occur incessantly. We cannot therefore take responsibility for facts, prices, addresses and circumstances in general that are constantly subject to alteration. Our guides are updated on a regular basis as we reprint, and we are always grateful to readers who let us know of any errors, changes or serious omissions they come across.

Text: David Henderson
Photography: Ken Walsh and David Henderson, M.M.P.A.; pp.19, 53, 58 Claude Huber
We wish thank the Spanish National Tourist Office in Geneva for their help in the preparation of this guide. We are also grateful to Nick Inman, Clara Villanueva, Prudence Smith and Jane Wishart.
Cartography: 🔵 Falk-Verlag, Hamburg.

Contents

Maps

The Region and the People

A thousand years ago, the Moors reckoned that the Costa Blanca was a paradise, a fragment from the next world that had fortunately fallen onto this one. They had a point. Ten months a year, a blazing sun warms beaches, ochre plains and misty, wind-sculptured mountains. Olive, eucalyptus and carob trees dot ancient fields. Orange groves fill the valleys and in January and February the mountains burst into colour with the pink and white of almond blossoms.

Spain's fabulous "White Coast" was christened 2,500 years ago by Greek traders, who founded the colony of *Akra Leuka*, White Headland, on a site near today's Alicante. The Romans called the provincial capital *Lucentum*, City of Light. The letters "A.L." and "L.A." (*Lucentum Alicante*) are proudly displayed on Alicante's city crest.

But the exceptional tourist potential of the Costa Blanca's sun, sea and mountains remained unexploited until the early 1960s, when *alicantinos* looked north to the Costa Brava and south at the Costa del Sol and suddenly realized that they could offer something just as good, if not better. From that moment, *el boom*, as the local people call it, was inevitable. Benidorm, once populated by fishermen as proficient at smuggling as catching sardines, sprouted scores of hotels and hundreds of apartments and villas, with beds enough for more than 500,000 guests. A four-lane superhighway (with minor interruptions) follows the coast from the French frontier as far as Alicante, and every year several million tourists speed along it to the burgeoning resorts.

Merely defining the Costa Blanca calls for a word about contemporary Spanish politics. Since the restoration of democracy and the decentralization of power, the *comunidades autónomas* (regional governments) have taken over their own touristic destiny. The name "Costa Blanca", hitherto a generality, now belongs exclusively to the authorities in Valencia. The coast from San Pedro del Pinatar to Aguilas, pertaining to Murcia, is

Graceful sweep of Benidorm's beaches—pride of Costa Blanca.

officially known as the Costa Cálida. The southern-most strip is now called the Costa del Almería. This book touches on all three regions, and even ventures into a corner of the Costa del Azahar.

But the visitor is rarely aware of these subtleties on the strangely beautiful coastline extending from beachy Denia to Cape Gata, via the tourist metropolis of Benidorm and the bustling port of Alicante. On the southern stretch of the coast, the Mar Menor offers superb facilities and natural wonders, and beyond historic Cartagena lie the unspoilt beaches of Garrucha—a campers' paradise.

Inland there are winding country roads that climb hillsides first terraced by the Moors, serving picturesque villages unchanged for centuries. Enter the impressive Moorish fortress of

Guadalest through a tunnel excavated more than a thousand years ago and still the only way in. At Elche, a favourite excursion spot, thousands of palm trees, originally planted by the Carthaginians, form Europe's largest date-palm forest. It is rivalled by only one other, 30 kilometres away at Orihuela, a charming town on the banks of the River Segura.

For lovers of the past, there are fine examples of the great ages of Spanish art and architecture, starting with the exceptional Bronze Age gold artefacts on display in Villena. Examples of Francisco Salzillo's baroque polychrome wood sculpture are to be found in almost every church in his native province of Murcia and the processional figures carved by the modern Valen-

Swimming and sun-blinds keep visitors cool in the summer heat.

cian sculptor, Mariano Benlliure, bring many visitors to the village of Crevillente at Easter.

Entertainments for everybody are within easy reach on the Costa Blanca. You can try your hand at an endless variety of sports: bowling, water-skiing, wind-surfing, scuba-diving, tennis and golf; or see top matadors fight in *corridas* in the major towns. There are gargantuan barbecues where you can feast with more than a thousand other guests. And nature's attractions complement the exciting night-life of Benidorm and Alicante from dusk to dawn. There's even a safari park, where giraffes roam free in the Spanish wilds.

Spain is celebrated for its fiestas, and one of the most spectacu-

The land of plenty: almond blossoms, oranges and a quiet life.

lar is Villajoyosa's "Moors and Christians" extravaganza with its re-enacting of old rivalrics. Even more dramatic is Alicante's famous *Hogueras de San Juan* in June, in which giant effigies are burned at midnight, a legacy from a pagan, mid-summer sacrifice to the fire gods.

Although tourism is the major industry now in this area, agriculture thrives on reliable underground water supplies and age-old crafts continue to flourish. Paper, shoes, toys and dolls are profitable exports, and lace, cane and esparto grass-work are important cottage industries. At Jijona, factories continue to make *turrón*—a honey and almond sweet—much in the same way as the Moors once did. Torrevieja's ancient salt industry remains one of Europe's largest.

The peoples of Valencia, Alicante, Murcia and Almería speak a bewildering variety of dialects: *valenciano, lemosín, alicantino* and *murciano*. The "local" languages are growing in importance; even street and road signs use them. But everyone speaks Castilian, Spain's official language, too. Learn a few words and doors will open to you—it's that kind of place.

A Brief History

Nothing has had a greater impact on the Costa Blanca than foreign invasion: Iberians, Phoenicians, Greeks, Romans, Visigoths and Moors had moulded Spain's Mediterranean shores centuries before international tourism gained a foothold. But before any of these were the Costa Blanca's first inhabitants. Known as Neanderthal men, they lived primitively and spent a large part of their time hunting. Then, as the Stone Age came to an end, short, dark-skinned Iberians started to make their way from North Africa to the Spanish Peninsula. These fierce fighters skilled in guerrilla warfare roamed the Mediterranean foothills, painting a vivid record of their battles on the walls of their rock shelters.

The Celts began to flood into Spain from the north sometime after 900 B.C. They settled in the north and west of the country, never penetrating as far as the Costa Blanca. In central Spain they were slowly absorbed by the reluctant Iberians, but elsewhere both tribes kept fiercely apart, establishing from the first the renowned independence that still characterizes Spain's provinces.

Early Traders

The Phoenicians ventured across the Mediterranean from present-day Lebanon, reaching Spain by about 1100 B.C. They founded many trading settlements in the "remote" or "hidden land" they named *Span* or *Spania*. The Costa Blanca was soon dotted with such Phoenician towns as Elche and Játiva.

After about 650 B.C., Greek traders arrived on the coast to compete for Spain's rich mineral deposits and fertile land. The influence of Greece was short-lived, although the olive and the grape, a Greek legacy, are cultivated in the region.

The Carthaginians, a people related to the Phoenicians, came from North Africa and subsequently took over much of southern Spain, beginning with Cádiz in 501 B.C. The town had sought help from the Carthaginian army in its war against local tribes, and the "invited guest" decided to stay. The main centre of Carthaginian power in Spain was sited on the Costa Blanca: Carthago Nova, now Cartagena, followed in prominence by Alicante.

Carthage, challenged by Rome in the First Punic War (264–241 B.C.), lost most of her neglected holdings in Spain through Iberian attacks. But Carthage's luck changed with an initial victory in the Second Punic War (218–201 B.C.). Hannibal, the Carthaginian general, led one of history's greatest military marches the length of the Costa Blanca to France and Italy, crossing the Pyrenees and the Alps, in the hope of surprising an unsuspecting Rome. The Romans riposted by invading Spain to cut off Hannibal's supply route and stayed there 600 years.

Under Roman Rule

It took the Romans almost 300 years to subdue the Iberian tribes. Outpost duty was decidedly unpopular with the legionaries, but the Roman army finally prevailed.

There's no doubt that the Roman presence in Spain had a great influence on the country, bringing the gifts of engineering and architecture. Stability and unity were promoted by the introduction of Latin, from which modern Spanish developed,

Almanzora's caves have sheltered Neanderthalers and gypsies alike.

Roman law, still the basis of Spain's legal system, and, eventually, Christianity.

But the Roman empire, overstretched and increasingly corrupt, began to crumble. The Romans withdrew from Spain, leaving the country to be overrun by various barbarian tribes, especially the Vandals. These tribes were eventually subdued by the Visigoths, who controlled much of southern Spain for some 300 years. But they did not integrate, nor did they learn the lessons of history, and in a palace intrigue, one faction invited the Moors into the country as their allies.

Moorish Domination

In A.D. 711, the Arab chief Tariq landed at Gibraltar with 12,000 Berber troops. Thus began an 800-year epoch of Christian opposition to the newly arrived Moslems. The Moors—the name commonly given to all Moslems in Spain—carried all before them. Within ten years their green, crescent standard flew over most of Spain. Kartajanah, Mursiyah and Xativa are still known by their Moorish names.

The Moors were relatively tolerant rulers and taxed non-believers rather than trying to convert them. They introduced the manufacture of paper, which is carried on today in Játiva. They laid out a system of irrigation still in use in the Guadalest Valley and filled the *huertas* (orchards) of the Costa Blanca with oranges, peaches and pomegranates. Rice, cotton and sugar cane were also first cultivated on Spanish soil by the Moors.

Numerous Moorish fortifications on the Costa Blanca survive to this day, and the pottery of the region still reflects the influence of Moorish craftsmen. Learning was considerably advanced by the Moors, and a medical treatise written by an Arab physician in Crevillente is recognized today as revolutionary for its time.

The Tide Turns

But like the Visigoths, the Moors ignored history. Feeling the rising strength of Christianity, and weakened by constant fighting among themselves, they sought outside help from the Almohades. These fanatical Berber warriors from present-day Morocco quickly reduced Moorish Spain to a province of their North African empire, endowing it with enough strength to resist the Christian forces awhile longer.

Fruit trees bring life to an arid mountain village.

Fortunes swayed to and fro for centuries, but it was not until 1212, at Las Navas de Tolosa in northern Spain, that the Chris-tians gained their first decisive victory. The Christian provinces gradually captured and annexed former bastions of Moorish rule: Ferdinand III conquered Murcia for Castile in 1242; Denia and Já-tiva fell to James the Conqueror of Aragon in 1244, though it was **15** not until 1265 that he secured Cartagena. The Moors were on the retreat, withdrawing to the almost impregnable mountain fortress area of Granada, where they held out until 1492.

The Golden Age

Spain's golden century began under the "Catholic Monarchs", a title conferred by Pope Alexander VI on Ferdinand II and Isabella, who united the country under the Christian kingdoms of Aragon and Castile after the fall of Granada in 1492. That same eventful year, Columbus, seeking a western route to the East on behalf of the Catholic Monarchs, discovered America. And Ferdinand and Isabella consolidated Christian rule by decreeing that all Jews—the banking and business experts—must adopt Catholicism or be exiled. The Moors —the source of cheap labour and

MAS, Barcelona

vital agricultural know-how—were given the same alternative in 1502.

The Segura Valley was the last part of Spain to be inhabited by Moslems, who abandoned their fortresses there in 1505. As the Inquisition established its reign of terror to stamp out heresy, converted Jews, *conversos*, and Moslems, *moriscos*, were looked upon with suspicion, and many left the country or were condemned to death. Agricultural productivity was to suffer considerably after the official expulsion of the *moriscos* in 1609.

The conquest of the New World brought Spain fame and immense wealth, especially under Charles I and Philip II, but much was squandered and wasted; slowly the decline set in. In 1588, the immensely powerful but badly led Armada set out to invade England, only to be beaten by Drake and a providential storm. Another important defeat took place at Rocroi, in Flanders, in 1643, when Spanish troops, never to regain their former glory, were routed by the French.

Ferdinand and Isabella, who united Spain in 1492.

French Ascendancy

Spanish internal affairs became the concern of other great powers after Charles II died in 1700 without heirs. The Archduke Charles of Austria rivalled France's Philip of Bourbon, designated to ascend the throne, in the ensuing War of the Spanish Succession. On the Costa Blanca, Murcia was defended from the invasion of Archduke Charles by its bishop, with the help of local people, and Játiva fought the succession of Philip so fiercely that when resistance was finally overcome in 1707, the town's name was changed to San Felipe; the former name was not to be restored until the 19th century. Philip finally gained the Spanish throne under the terms of the Treaty of Utrecht in 1713.

Nearly a hundred years later, during the Napoleonic wars, Spanish ships fought alongside the French fleet against Lord Nelson at Cape Trafalgar, southeast of Cádiz. But as the wars continued, Napoleon, distrustful of his ally, forced the Spanish king to abdicate in 1808 and imposed his brother Joseph as king of Spain. He sent thousands of troops across the Pyrenees to subdue the Spaniards, who then **17** revolted. Aided by British troops subsequently commanded by the Duke of Wellington, they drove the French out of the Iberian peninsula. Denia, held by the enemy, was blockaded for eight months in 1813. What the world knows as the Peninsular War (1808–14) is referred to in Spain as the War of Independence, and the country's first, though short-lived, constitution was drafted during this period.

From Decline to Chaos

Hopes of setting up a constitutional monarchy were quickly dashed, and Spain was plunged into a century of power struggles at home. Overseas, her American colonies revolted and gained independence. Soon there was little left of the once great Spanish empire, and an attempt in 1873 to form a republic failed. In 1902, Alfonso XIII took up his duties as king at the age of 16. His reign was a difficult time for Spain. Prosperity and stability evaded the country, which remained neutral during World War I.

In 1923, assailed by economic problems and with catastrophe imminent, the king accepted a general, Miguel Primo de Rivera, as dictator. Six years later the op-

position of radical forces resulted in Primo de Rivera's fall. Neither reform nor the maintenance of order seemed possible. In 1931 the king himself went into exile following anti-royalist election results, and another republic was founded.

Parliamentary democracy was impeded by the ideological commitment of various political factions and compromise was rare. There was a succession of right-wing attempts to govern and Spain floundered in a sea of political strikes and violence. Then the Left won the 1936 elections and was immediately in violent collision with the Right.

In July 1936, a large section of the army under General Francisco Franco rose in revolt against the government. On Franco's side were monarchists, conservatives, the Church and the right-wing Falangists. Against him was a collection of republicans, liberals, socialists, communists and anarchists. The ensuing Civil War became one of the great crusades of the 20th century. Germany and Italy supplied

Splendid vista from Alicante's Castillo de Santa Bárbara.

Franco's Nationalists with arms and air power, and the Soviet Union gave aid to Spain's communists.

To many people in Europe, often unaware of, or indifferent to, the particular Spanish origins of the struggle, the Civil War was seen as a crucial conflict between democracy and dictatorship, or, from the other side, as one of law and order against social revolution and chaos. The bloodshed lasted for three years and cost hundreds of thousands of lives.

Even when the war ended, the hardship continued. But Generalísimo Franco, Spain's new

caudillo (leader), despite Hitler's efforts at persuasion, succeeded in keeping his exhausted country out of World War II.

Architect's dream come true in this high-rise development.

Modern Times

During the years of post-war reconstruction, Franco encouraged tourism on a grand scale. Profoundly affecting the economy and the people, this transformed Spain's most attractive coasts, though not always for the better.

When the *caudillo* (leader) died in 1975, Prince Juan Carlos, the grandson of the Bourbon King Alfonso XIII, succeeded to the Spanish throne. The new king firmly led the way from totalitarianism to democracy. A new constitution granted wide-ranging powers to the regions. In 1986 Spain entered the European Community, ending decades of isolation. On the domestic scene, troubles like inflation, unemployment, crime and pollution precluded overconfidence. But the new Spain was firmly back in Europe's mainstream.

Where to Go

With such a long stretch of coast to cover and so many historic towns to visit inland, the Costa Blanca may seem difficult to get around in—particularly if you don't have a car. But the itineraries in the following pages take in all the tourist-worthy sights in this sprawling region and every one of these important places of interest can easily be reached by public transport.

Most visitors will be staying within easy reach of Alicante so our trips start out from here. At the centre of the region's road network, Alicante is also a logical base for motorists and for train and bus connections. Tourists who fly into Alicante's airport on package holidays usually begin their sightseeing with a visit to the provincial capital.

From Alicante we head north along the coast to Gandia and south to Cartagena. We then make for the historic inland towns of Elche, Orihuela and Murcia, equally within easy reach.

Benidorm is the main destination for many tourists and this popular town provides another good point of departure for excursions to nearby islands like the Isla de Benidorm, as well as to moody villages like Guadalest, in the interior.

The southernmost stretch of coast south of Cartagena is not readily accessible by bus or train. But motorists as well as adventurers willing to brave infrequent, capricious transport services will enjoy discovering the few remaining pockets of unspoilt, arid beauty and remote whitewashed villages. Most of this coast, though, is filling with hotels, villas and apartment blocks.

The Essentials

There are certain sights no visitor to the Costa Blanca should miss. If time presses and you have to make a choice, bear in mind these highlights:

Alicante
Castillo de Santa Bárbara

North Coast
Villajoyosa
Benidorm
Guadalest

South Coast
Cartagena
Mojácar

Inland
Elche
Orihuela Cathedral
Catedral de Santa Maria and Museo Salzillo (Murcia)

Getting Around

By train

For information, contact the Information Office of RENFE, Avenue Salamanca, Alicante (tel. 592 02 02).

The principal rail lines are: Valencia–Alicante–Cartagena; Alicante–Madrid; Alicante–Denia (along the coast); Cartagena–Murcia–Albacete–Madrid.

By coach

A cheap, though ' not always comfortable, method of travel. Coaches link Alicante to Benidorm and Cartagena, as well as to Murcia, Denia and Alcoy.

The main coach station in Alicante is in Calle Portugal, 17 (tel. 513 07 00).

By car

The important routes are: N-340 (Barcelona–Alicante–Murcia–Cádiz); N-332 (Valencia–Alicante–Almería, by the coast); N-330 (Alicante–Albacete); N-301 (Cartagena–Murcia–Madrid); A-7 (Alicante–Valencia–Barcelona).

By air

There are flights to the major Spanish cities, but there are few regional connections.

Alicante

Swaying palms and luminous skies, along with some of Spain's best restaurants and *tapa* bars, lure visitors to the provincial capital of Alicante. The town is as popular with European holiday-makers today as it was with Greek and Roman colonizers in ancient times.

You'll always see cosmopolitan crowds here, especially on the **Explanada de España**, the splendid waterfront promenade which stretches alongside the harbour, and on the Paseo Maritimo. You can stroll to the music of the municipal band on Sundays or try one of the restaurants on the Paseo. Just east of the Explanada an irresistible stretch of sandy beach, the Playa del Postiguet, beckons.

The broad **Rambla de Méndez Núñez**, running at right angles to the Explanada, is good for a morning's shopping and has a lively market at one end. It's also the route taken by patriotic, civic and religious processions, most notably the *Hogueras de San Juan* parade held every June. Off the *rambla* (the name given to a broad, tree-lined avenue) to the right is the Calle Mayor, a pedestrian street. Here, street vendors hawk pens, watches and jewellery, and on religious holdays processions pass by on their way from the **Catedral de San Nicolás de Bari**. Situated a stone's throw from the Calle Mayor on Avenida General Sanjurjo in the old town, the cathedral was considerably restored after the Civil War. Note the impressive nave and façade, excellent examples of Juan de Herrera's austere style, recalling the magnificent Escorial Palace near Madrid, which he also designed.

Walk beyond the Calle Mayor and the tranquil Plaza de Santa Faz to get to the Plaza del Ayuntamiento, where a coin and stamp market is held on Sundays and public holidays. The square is the site of the **Ayuntamiento** (Town Hall) with its beautiful Baroque façade, designed in the 18th century by Lorenzo Chápuli, a local architect. A highly polished brass stud on the first step of the main staircase registers a height exactly three metres above sea level. This is Spain's official altitude-measuring point. The handsome, red-lettered marble plaque on the same staircase is a copy of the city's charter, presented by Ferdinand II of Aragon in 1490.

The Ayuntamiento houses a small picture gallery and a chapel with tiles from Manises, an important Valencian ceramics centre. Look for the painting of the patron saint of Alicante, Saint Nicholas of Bari, over the altar. There are 18th-century royal

Cherubs, angels and saints in baroque extravaganza on the façade of Iglesia de Santa Maria.

portraits in the Salón Azul (Blue Room) and archives which preserve the document of privileges granted to the city by Alfonso X, the Wise, in the 13th century.

A short distance uphill brings you to the baroque west front of the **Iglesia de Santa María** (between the Calle Mayor and the Calle Jorge Juan). The church dates from the 14th century. This is one of many churches built during the Christianization of territory won from the Moors by James I in legendary 13th-century battles; it stands on the site of a mosque. Works by Braque, Chagall, Giacometti, Picasso and many other 20th-century artists hang next door in the **Museo de Arte del Siglo XX** (Museum of 20th-Century Art).

Beyond you'll find the tiny **Barrio de Santa Cruz**. This quarter is all that remains of the *Villa Vieja*, or old town. You can still see fascinating glimpses of traditional narrow streets, where houses are decorated with potted plants and wrought-iron grilles.

From this *barrio* you'll be able to see the most prominent

Finding Your Way			
Ascensor	lift, elevator	*Isla*	island
Autopista	motorway	*Jardin*	garden
Avenida	avenue	*Mercado*	market
Ayuntamiento	town hall	*Muelle*	docks
Barrio	quarter	*Murallas*	city walls
Caho	cape	*Oficina de Turismo*	tourist office
Calle	street		
Carretera	road	*Paseo*	boulevard
Castillo	castle	*Playa*	beach
Catedral	cathedral	*Plaza de toros*	bull ring
Ciudad vieja	old city	*Puerto*	harbour
Correos	post office	*Rambla*	boulevard
Cueva	cave	*Río*	river
Estación de ferrocarril	railway station	*Ruinas*	ruins
		Sierra	mountain range
		Vía	avenue
Faro	lighthouse	*Derecha*	right
Fortaleza	fortress	*Izquierda*	left
Iglesia	church	*Todo derecho*	straight ahead

VALENCIA

MAR

MEDITERRANEO

300 m

300 yards

Ascensor

Castillo de
Santa Bárbara

BARRIO DE
SANTA CRUZ

Iglesia de
Santa María

Paseito Ramiro

Playa del postiguet

Puerta del Mar

Avenida de Jovellanos

Catedral de
San Nicolás de Bari

Ayuntamiento

Calle Mayor

Calle Jorge Juan

Pl. de Santa
Faz

C.
General Sanjurjo

Calle de San Fernando

Calle Mayor

Ayuntamiento

Calle Altamira

Puerto

Rambla de Méndez Núñez

Explanada de España

Paseo Conde Vallellano

Av.
de la Constitución

Mercado

Calle Cienfuegos

Avenida de Alfonso X el Sabio

Calle de Gerona

Calle de San Francisco

Plaza de
Gabriel
Miró

Calle de San Fernando

Calle de las Navas

Calle General Goded

Calle de Pascual Pérez

Calle de Colón

Correos

N

Plaza
Calvo
Sotelo

Calle Canalejas

Avenida Ramón y Cajal

Parque de Canalejas

Av. del Doctor Gadea

Plaza de
los
Luceros

Av. Federico Soto

Museo
Arqueológico
Provincial

Avenida
General Mola

Calle G. O'Donnell

Avenida de Maisonnave

Calle de los Reyes Católicos

C. General Lacy

C. Portugal

C. Lorenzo Casanova

C. Alemania

Calle Italia

C. López

C. Portugal

ALICANTE

MURCIA

Alicante's fortress, the Castillo de Santa Bárbara, rises above peaceful orchards. Smiling faces are normal in the countryside here.

 sight in Alicante, the historic **Castillo de Santa Bárbara**, perched 350 feet above the city on Mount Benacantil. The site has been fortified since prehistoric times and offers beautiful views of Aitana. San Juan, Santa Pola and Benidorm and Tabarca islands in the distance. To get to the castle, drive up the winding road to the summit or use the lift at the far end of Calle Juan Bautista Lafora, close to Postiguet beach. Santa Bárbara, built by the Carthaginians in the 3rd century B.C., was so well forti-

fied that for nearly 2,000 years nobody conquered it. Only when the French, during the War of the Spanish Succession in 1707, succeeded in blowing up part of the garrison was the castle taken.

On the opposite side of town in the Barrio San Blas is the smaller **Castillo de San Fernando**, begun during the War of Independence (1808–14). The castle, set above the trees of the small **Parque Municipal**, provides a favourite spot for viewing Santa Bárbara and the port in the late afternoon.

The **Museo Arqueológico Provincial** in the Diputación (Chamber of Deputies) at 6 Avenida de la Estacion contains an interesting ceramics collection, with some pieces dating back to the Greeks. Be sure to take a look at the graceful pottery of the **27**

Iberians, adorned with simple painted lines. You'll also be able to admire the Stone Age pottery and bone bracelets, as well as Carthaginian and Greek carvings and Moorish relics.

Outskirts of Alicante

Outside town, on the main Valencia highway, the **Monasterio de Santa Verónica** (St. Veronica's Monastery) attracts about 15,000 pilgrims and a good many hawkers during the annual May celebration of the *Santa Faz* (Holy Face). Armed with canes decorated with bunches of rosemary, the participants proceed on foot to the monastery, where they venerate the Holy Face cloth that, according to tradition, retained the bloodstained image of Jesus' face after Saint Veronica used it to wipe his brow as he went to Calvary.

The sacred relic was first worshipped in the Alicante region during a drought in 1489. As it was being carried across the site of the present-day monastery, the *Santa Faz* is said to have suddenly become too heavy to hold and believers claim that a tear fell from the right eye of the image. This was interpreted as a sign to construct the building which has housed the cloth ever since. It can be seen at the high altar or in a chapel off the sacristy.

There are two other Holy Face handkerchiefs—one in Jaén and the other in the Vatican. According to Roman Catholic authorities, the original cloth was divided into three.

The small, flat island of **Nueva Tabarca** lies about an hour by boat from Alicante.* You won't see any pirates here, as the last of them sailed away from their former stronghold in 1786. But you will find fishermen, many of whom are direct descendants of some 600 Genoese mercenaries King Charles III rescued from captivity on Tunisia's Tabarka Island, hence the name. These people have made Nueva Tabarca their home for more than two centuries, in spite of poor fishing and the lack

An Alicante landmark—treelined Explanada de España lines dock.

* From mid-April to October, boats run daily from Alicante and Santa Pola (whence the sea voyage takes half as long). There is no service in winter.

of doctor, priest and schoolmaster. It was tourism that finally saved the declining population from fading away altogether and provided islanders with a priest and teacher at last. Sun-seeking visitors, mostly Spaniards, flock to the island on Sundays, the most popular day for excursions. Even then, you'll always be able to find peace and quiet on a tiny, seaweed-draped cove beyond the main sandy bay.

Inland from Alicante

For a change of scenery, drive north of Alicante into the rocky, lunar-like landscape of the Cabeço d'Or mountains. This is where you'll find the **Cuevas de Canalobre** (Candelabrum Cave), which is reached by following the N-340 from San Juan de Alicante until the turn-off for BUSOT, where signs mark the way to the cave. Floodlights dramatize the eerie ranks of gigantic stalagmites and stalactites which crowd chambers up to 350 feet high. The acoustics are so exceptional that summer concerts are held in the caves.

Jijona also lies within easy reach of the provincial capital. This town, just 27 kilometres from Alicante on the N-340, is renowned for the manufacture of *turrón*, an exotic sweet of Moorish origin, made from ground almonds, orange-blossom honey, egg white and sugar. Traditionally served by the Spanish at Christmas time, the flat bars of *turrón* are very hard. A softer, sweeter version called *torta de turrón* is oval and made with extra honey and whole almonds.

You can learn all about this popular confection on a tour of El Lobo factory, founded in 1725. There's even a small museum on the premises.

From Jijona, continue along the N-340 to **Alcoy** (56 km. from Alicante). Don't be disappointed by this grey industrial town, for it manufactures some of Spain's most popular sweets. They are *peladillas*, Marcona almonds coated with sugar. Sometimes pine kernels are sugar-coated, too, and the delicious result is called *pinyonets*.

Although Alcoy has a reputation for dourness and occasional winter snow, the towns-people are usually very friendly. At the annual celebration of the Moors and Christians fiesta, for example, you'll be astonished by the colourful costumes and lively

The bell towers and church domes, sunshine and simple houses of Alcoy hide a secret all their own—peladillas—Spain's most succulent sweet.

faces. If you're here out of season, the costumes, worn year after year, will be on display in the 18th-century Casal de San Jordi.

The **Museo Camilo Visedo** near by houses a fascinating collection of Iberian clay sculpture taken from a settlement in the Sierra Serreta. To visit the site, just a few kilometres from town, take the C-3313 road, but prepare yourself for a hard 30-minute scramble up the Serreta.

From IBI onwards you'll see many castles and forts, some of them visible for miles. They were strategically positioned by ever-vigilant Romans, Moors and Christians.

The castle of CASTALLA, just off the Ibi-Villena road, is one of the most dramatically sited in Spain. It was built by the counts

Sax Castle, a powerful Roman fortification designed to withstand the heaviest attacks, stands as mute testimony to the fallen empire.

of Castalla but left incomplete. Further along the Villena road is the round castle of BIAR, of Moorish origin and still in reasonable condition. It was declared a national monument and is interesting both outside and in, especially the vaulted ceiling on the upper floor.

Continue now to the town of VILLENA, the farthest point from Alicante (64 km. away) on this tour. The **castle** here, noted for its double walls and high, eight-turreted tower, rarely found south of Madrid, also has national monument status. Villena's castle was originally built by Moors, though considerable additions were made in the 15th century. The town's priceless Bronze Age **treasure**, discovered in a clay jar in the riverbed, is exhibited in the Ayuntamiento (Town Hall). The gold jewellery and objects attest to the artistry of Villena's early inhabitants.

Swing south from Villena along the N-330 to SAX, site of the Roman town of Saxum. The towers of the original Roman castle, which has been fully restored, are still a look-out point. car on the new motorway. Back on the N-330 you soon come to PETREL's Moorish castle, reputed to have fabulous treasure buried in its grounds.

Unrestored medieval fortresses are found along the C-3212 road to ELDA, and beyond, at MONOVAR. Elda itself is noted for excellent wine and lace-making. The town was the birthplace of the famous writer, José Martínez Ruiz, better known as Azorín (see p. 29). From Elda, follow the signs to NOVELDA to find yet another Moorish castle set high on a hill. This one is the **Castillo de la Mola**, erected on the site of a Roman fort. It has an unusual tri-angular tower dating from the 13th century. Right next to it you'll see a strange structure reminiscent of Gaudí's still unfinished Templo de la Sagrada Familia in Barcelona.

If, after all this castle-viewing, you still haven't had enough, a few kilometres farther on in ASPE, you'll find *las ruinas* (the ruins). Local people will direct you to the castle, which they never call by that name. Look out for Roman and Moorish relics, which are still sometimes discovered here. Then make your way back to Alicante, just 28 kilometres away.

33

The North Coast

The Costa Blanca's growing reputation for magnificent beaches and lively resorts comes from the northern stretch of coast. Take the N-332 from Alicante and drive through CAMPELLO to the small fishing port of **Villajoyosa**. This picturesque village, some 30 kilometres from the provincial capital, is more authentically Spanish in character than Benidorm, its cosmopolitan neighbour.

Wind your way towards the sea through the narrow streets of the old town, and suddenly you'll see a group of housefronts in sun-bleached blues, pinks and yellows. White-rimmed doors and windows, black wrought-iron grilles, green blinds, and a massive Gothic church give the impression of a sparkling diadem—but then Villajoyosa literally means "Jewelled Town".

La Vila, as Villajoyosa is affectionately called, boasts some Roman, Moorish and Visigothic remains and Spain's oldest chocolate factories. But it's the vivacious Moors and Christians fiesta, with its bare-bellied, flashing-eyed "slave-girls" and swashbuckling "corsairs", that really makes the town unique. In the last week of July, many of the town's 16,000 inhabitants parade and fight in richly costumed companies—*los piratas, los tuareg* and *los moros del Rif* among them—re-enacting the defeat in 1538 of the Algerian pirate Zala Arráez, a Mediterranean scourge who started it all by sacking the castle in a daring dawn raid.

If you dress the part and stay on your feet for the seven days the fiesta lasts, you can join the ranks of *Els Pollosos*. This means "the Lousy Ones" in the *valeciano* dialect and refers to a "mercenary" company open to all volunteers. As a member of this group, you can take part in the famous Moorish attack, still faithfully acted out as it really happened over 4½ centuries ago. What with all the cannon firing and colourful acting, the excitement can reach fever pitch.

Benidorm, one of Spain's most famous resorts, lies just 12 kilometres north of Villajoyosa. On the way, you'll pass the Casino Costa Blanca, where the stakes are low and the excitement runs high. For an account of its discovery by world tourism and a description of the town's most interesting sights, see page 45.

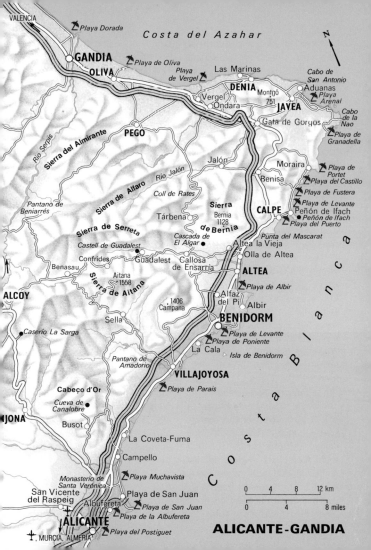

Altea, 10 kilometres north of Benidorm, was an important Phoenician port. The Moors called it Altaya, meaning "Health for All", but not before they had destroyed the first settlement and rebuilt the town. Altea is one of Spain's most memorable and tranquil towns, and a careful development policy helps to keep it that way. You'll find small bungalows here, rather than hotel blocks, and a delightful seaside market held on Tuesdays—a welcome and colourful change from supermarket monotony.

The 257 steps that climb steeply above the main shopping street, the Avenida Fermín Sanz Orrio, lead to the old village. Here the streets are almost always full of people, who congregate in local bars and restaurants. Altea boasts a number of art galleries and an artists' colony well-known in the region.

On Sundays and fiestas, in the afternoon, traditional games of *pelota* are played in the narrow streets near Altea's church square. Players strike the ball with their bare hands against walls, doors and windows—which are protected by grilles.

The best of the local beaches, most of which are pebbly, is south at ALBIR, between Altea and the Sierra Helada.

Calpe's popularity with tourists is ensured by two fine sandy beaches. This former fishing village (12 kilometres from Altea) lies at the base of the **Peñón de Ifach,** a volcanic rock thrusting out of the sea to a height of over 1,000 feet.

You don't have to be a mountaineer to climb the rock; anyone fit can make it to the top of this coastal landmark. On the way up, you can admire the wild flowers, and in autumn and winter you may catch sight of Audouin's Gull (a rare species with dark olive legs and a black-banded red bill). It's a good idea to take a jersey and something to drink.

If you have time, follow the coastal road from Calpe to MORAIRA, where flats and villas fill terraced hillsides high above rocky coves. Otherwise, take the main Alicante–Valencia road, which passes inland through rich agricultural country to GATA DE GORGOS—a town noted for cane and basket-work and even furniture—and rural Jávea.

Altea's delicately tiled roofs date from an age of skilled craftsmen.

Jávea, 27 kilometres from Calpe, sprawls between pine-covered Cape Nao to the south and Cape San Antonio to the north. The town is ideal for a quiet family holiday, especially in spring, when Jávea is magical with the scents of lemon and orange blossoms. Citrus fruit became the region's principal cash crop around the turn of the century when grain and the 17th-century windmills of Cape San Antonio were abandoned. Jávea has been proclaimed "environmentally nearly perfect" and you can bask in the Costa Blanca's brightest sunshine here. Jávea also has an interesting Museo Histórico y Etnográfico with an important collection of Iberian finds from Sierra de Montgó, and two strongly contrasting churches—an early 16th-century fortified building and a modern, boatshaped structure.

Ten kilometres from Jávea is **Denia,** with long sandy beaches, a lofty brooding castle and 2,500 feet of Mount Montgó to climb. On a clear day you can see all the way to Ibiza, 100 kilometres away. This town is another good centre for a family holiday. Once the Phoenicians unsuccessfully prospected for minerals here and the Greeks established a port. Today's growing industrial town, a centre of wood, plastics and toy making, takes its name from a Roman temple to Diana, the remains of which are on view in the Ayuntamiento. Just east of Denia, you can visit the Cueva de Agua Dulce (Freshwater Cave) with its two lakes. A little farther

Wrought-iron grilles decorate house façades in Altea (left); the Peñón de Ifach crowns the sea with splendour (below).

los Duques (Palace of the Dukes of Gandía), home of Saint Francis Borja (1510–72), fourth Duke of Gandía, who abandoned worldly pleasures to join the Jesuit order after the death of his wife. The palace, now a Jesuit college, is open to visitors. Guided tours, several times per day in season, visit apartments with superbly tiled floors, and the Duke's private chapel.

Inland from Gandía

From Gandía, the C-320, then the C-322 lead inland through orange groves, vineyards and slowly rising country to **Játiva** . This "city of a thousand fountains", huge plane trees and a sprawling fortress was probably founded by Hannibal in 219 B.C. Europe's first paper was made here in the 11th century. Both the painter José de Ribera and two infamous popes, Calixtus III and Alexander VI, were born in Játiva. The popes were members of the Borja family, better known to history as Italy's notorious Borgias.

Seek out Játiva's late-Renaissance **Colegiata** (Collegiate Church) in the Plaza de Calixto III. Just opposite is the **hospital,** ages old but still in use. It's noted

away near Vergel, you can try the well-kept **Safari Park** with animals galore, a fine dolphin show, children's amusement park and refreshments and restaurants.

At **Gandía** (32 km. north of Denia on the N-332), you'll be tempted to spend all your time on the town's broad promenades and 8 miles of splendid beaches. But it would be a pity to miss the quiet majesty of the **Palacio de**

The carved face on one of Játiva's thousand fountains is a blend of stone and water. Left: fisherman repairs net in sunny satisfaction.

for a splendid façade designed in the ornate 16th-century Plateresque style. Find time too for the well-presented **Museo Municipal** in Carrer de la Corretgeria, 46. In the courtyard round the corner, the 11th-century **Pila de los Moros** (Moorish Basin) once was used for traditional ablu-

tions. The figures decorating the basin are rarely seen in Muslim art, since Islam forbids human and animal representation.

Directly above the old town, the **Ermita de San Feliú** (Saint Felix's Hermitage) commands a wide view. Although it has been a Christian bastion since the 3rd

Bocairente village sprawls helter-skelter on its terraced hillside.

century, it was a pagan sacrificial site long before that. Continue uphill to the fortress, which is, in fact, two castles. Ramparts connect the smaller pre-Roman **Castillo Menor** (Small Castle) with the Roman and post-Roman **Castillo Mayor** (Main Castle),

once notorious for its dungeon. Disgraced princes and other noblemen were confined here, with the ruined 15th-century chapel adjacent for their only solace.

Leave Játiva on the C-340 and drive up into the highlands where thick-fleeced sheep and isolated farmhouses complete a memorable vista. Pass through ALBAIDA, known for its candle-making, and ONTENIENTE, an industrial

town, to picturesque **Bocairente**. with its narrow streets and charming old houses. Visit the village during late summer for the festival of folk dancing, or for February's Fiestas of Moors and Christians. Visit the sombre bull-ring that was hacked from solid rock for the *Corrida*.

For a town of barely 5,000 inhabitants, Bocairente's two small museums are impressive: the Museo Histórico (Historical Museum) is noted for a collection of Stone Age pottery, and the Museo Parroquial (Parish Museum) exhibits important paintings by Juan de Juanes, Ribalta and Sorolla. In the hills near by are Iberian cave tombs, referred to locally as the Covetes de Moros (Moorish Caves). Some were later lived in by hardy Christian holy men.

Benidorm

With twin, crescent-moon beaches, four miles of golden sands and an outstanding climate, Benidorm is one of Spain's most popular resorts. But it wasn't always so. Despite efforts over a hundred years ago by a local entrepreneur, who hoped to bring holiday-makers to the area by a regular stage coach service, large-scale tourism didn't come to Benidorm until the early 1960s. Since then, a mass of apartment blocks and hotels has sprung up and the town has become known as an international fun city. Some 250,000 people pack the place out in summer.

Love it or hate it, Benidorm is thoroughly cosmopolitan: restaurants here serve bacon and eggs, sauerkraut, smorgasbord and "tea like mother makes it". There are bars, cocktail lounges, sophisticated restaurants, modern hotels and a vast choice of discotheques and nightclubs. This makes for a happy, human, unending noise that contradicts

From mirador to market day: colourful contrasts in Benidorm, fun capital of the Costa Blanca.

those who say the town's name derives from the *valenciano* words for "sleep well".

The delightful **old village**, the size of a postage stamp, is tucked away on the long spur of land that divides the two beaches. A fort stood here until 1812, when British and Spanish troops blew it up while dislodging the French during Spain's War of Independence, leaving only ruins. The greatest concentration of shops and entertainments is to be found around the original village.

Away from the beaches there's no end to the amusements, whether you're keen on sun or shade, active or passive pursuits. You can go go-karting or ten-pin bowling, visit two parks and the pools and water slides of Aqualand. Or watch medieval jousting while dining on whole roast chicken, followed by dancing—if you're able.

The **Isla de Benidorm**, a wedge-shaped rock of an island you can see from any of Benidorm's beaches, is an unofficial bird sanctuary, uninhabited except for a summer bar. It's a good spot for a picnic and swim, although the water is deep. Boat trips from Benidorm average 20 minutes each way; make

arrangements to return on one of your boatman's later runs.

Inland from Benidorm

The mountains you see off in the distance on Benidorm's horizon are fragrant with wild herbs and lavender, and in July and August the hedges are lush with blackberries that few local people bother to pick. Drive south on the motorway to Villajoyosa, then take the road that leads to Sella. The countryside is undistinguished until suddenly you look down on the emerald-green waters of the Amadorio Dam, a favourite haunt of fishermen and discerning picnickers. Within another 5 kilometres you arrive at SELLA village, dwarfed beneath an extraordinary plateau.

From Sella the road winds higher through terraced hillsides filled with vines, until it reaches its highest point at PUERTO DE TUDONS (3,345 feet). About 8 kilometres on, a secondary road leads to PENAGUILA, an exquisite old Moorish village with a sturdy ruined castle.

Guadalest, one of the most impenetrable fortresses in Spain.

At BENASAU, the Sella road meets the C3313. To the west (16 km.) lies Alcoy (see pp. 30–31), to the east CONFRIDES, a picturesque mountain town.

Now make for **Guadalest** (some 10 km. to the east), the Costa Blanca's famed "eagle's nest" fortress, built by the Moors 1,200 years ago. Inaccessible except for a tunnel carved through 50 feet of solid rock, Guadalest was never conquered, though James I of Aragon took it by siege during the 13th-century Reconquest. The fortress even withstood an earthquake in 1644, as well as attempts by the Austrian Archduke Charles to blast his way in during the War of the Spanish Succession. Guadalest itself is just as spectacular as the view from it. Wandering round the compact castle, you'll understand why, for lack of space, the belfry had to be built outside, and why the picturesque old cemetery is so small.

From Guadalest, the road leads to the small town of CALLOSA DE ENSARRIA, centre of the honey industry, where you can taste before you buy, often six or eight different flavours. From Callosa take the Parcent road, follow it for 2½ kilometres

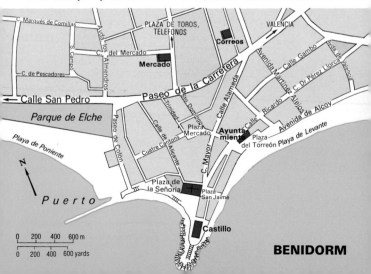

BENIDORM

and make a right-hand turn at the entrance to the **El Algar waterfalls**, a tumbling oasis beneath the massive Sierra Bernia formed by a tributary of the River Guadalest. Leave your car in the parking area and walk to the 80-foot falls. You can swim beneath them in chilly waters, then picnic by the cool, leafy pools above. It's easy to get away from crowds in this pleasant spot, but if you're in the mood for company, you'll find lots of people in the restaurants near the car park.

The next stop is TARBENA (10 km. farther along the C-3318), an invigorating mountain village famed for its delicious sausages. They're made from a secret recipe handed down to the present-day villagers by their Mallorcan ancestors, who came here in the early 17th century as part of an official repopulation scheme.

After Tárbena comes the finest scenery of all: bold, terraced mountains, wide undulating valleys and scattered farms connected by mule tracks. In spring the countryside is covered with the pink and white of almond blossoms, but the road is for all seasons, with groves of gnarled olive trees alongside it, their leaves blowing silver in the

An icy plunge in El Algar's rushing waters and the serene contemplation of the Tárbena landscape make for a perfect day on the Costa Blanca.

evening light. Follow the road to COLL DE RATES, 1,500 feet above the wide orange- and vine-filled plains that sweep up to Jávea, Denia, Gandía and the deep-blue Mediterranean. Farther on, take the road to JALON, where in late summer farmers sell muscat grapes to passers-by, and you can buy some of the strong local wine. Or carry on past Orba to Benidoleig and visit the prehistoric caves LAS CALAVERAS. Here high domed ceilings drip with stalagtites, and human bones more than 50 000 years old have been found.

Six kilometres more bring you to the Valencia–Alicante highway near Ondara.

The South Coast

The fishing port and resort of **Santa Pola** (18 km, south of Alicante on the N-332) has an extraordinary number of restaurants. Nearby waters, particularly rich in prawns and red mullet, provide all manner of eating houses, both on the beach and in the town, with some of the best seafood on the coast. There's also a 14th-century castle and several good beaches with fine, white sand.

Thousands of pines, palms and eucalyptus trees, planted to control shifting sand dunes, shade the beaches at **Guardamar del Segura** (17 km. south again on the N-332), an important fishing centre. Spiny lobsters are a speciality of Guardamar restaurants. From here, the road travels a further 15 kilometres, past the salt flats of La Mata, to Torrevieja.

The long-vanished "old tower" from which **Torrevieja** took its name has been replaced by a new one, built with funds raised by expatriate citizens. The expanding summer resort and its long, sandy beaches co-exist with Europe's largest and oldest salt industry. The enormous mountain of salt you'll see comes

from the La Mata and Torrevieja pans. Visitors are welcome Tuesdays and Thursdays from 5 p.m. Request passes from the office of the Nueva Compañía Arrendataria de las Salinas de Torrevieja on the port's main square. (Photography permits are harder to get.)

In August Torrevieja pulsates to the music of the *Habaneras* festival. The theme is the lively, song form of the same name (remember Bizet's *Carmen?*), brought back from Cuba during the 19th-century salt-export voyages. The festivities include musical competitions, concerts and shows by leading—sometimes international—companies.

On down the coast road we get to a string of growing resorts forming a summer holiday centre—La Zenia, Cabo Roig and Campoamor.

Another 10 kilometres to the south lies the natural wonder of the Costa Cálida, the **Mar Menor,** a salt water lagoon separated from the Mediterranean by two strips of land known collectively as La Manga. The shallow lagoon of some 80 square miles is calmer and saltier than the Mediterranean, so you sink less easily. It can also be several de-

All is shipshape in Cartagena's port and elegant streets.

grees warmer, which accounts for the thermal breezes and mellow summer temperatures. It's even mildly rich—and becoming richer—in mineral salts.

The Mar Menor is a sportsman's paradise. You can sign on for sailing, scuba-diving and wind-surfing courses and water-

ski on its tranquil waters. On shore there is considerable scope for tennis, or you can try clay-pigeon shooting. For golfers there are twin 18-hole Kentucky blue-grass courses, and the local golf club has a ranch which hires out mounts for riding.

The area of Mar Menor is also noted for its windmills, some of them restored to perfect working condition.

La Manga has been developed as a resort, with hotels and apartment blocks straddling the 14 miles of sand that separate the two seas. You'll find the Casino del Mar Menor in the Hotel Doblemar, halfway along La Manga. The mainland side of the lagoon boasts the smaller but thriving resorts of SANTIAGO DE LA RIBERA and LOS ALCAZARES, both of which are popular with service personnel from the air base inland at SAN JAVIER.

The compact, bustling city of **Cartagena** (26 kilometres south of Los Alcázares on the N-332) was a major naval port long before Saint James is said to have landed here with the Gospel in A.D. 36. Romans, Visigoths and Moors all squabbled over the strategically positioned town, which was sacked by Sir Francis **53**

Drake in 1588 and taken by Archduke Charles in 1707.

Head for the port and the large waterfront **Plaza del Ayuntamiento.** The big, grey, cigar-shaped object you'll see on view here is a submarine, built by the local inventor Isaac Peral and launched in 1888, ten years too late to make a world record.

Just north of the Plaza, take a coffee at one of the open-air cafés on the traffic-free Calle Mayor. Then head uphill to the **Castillo de la Concepción** at the highest point of the city. The castle dates back to Roman and perhaps even Carthaginian times. It's surrounded by the Parque de las Torres, a beautifully land-scaped vantage point. The pepper-pot lighthouse in the park, of Roman or Moorish origin, wrecked many a marauding ship when it was blacked out by Cartagena's defenders.

One glance over the almost landlocked harbour explains why Andrea Doria, the 16th-century Genoese admiral, remarked that the Mediterranean had only three safe ports: June, July and Cartagena. You'll also see why Carta-

A stiff breeze on a wind-surfer's sail sets the pace for the day.

gena is called the "City of Castles". Almost every hill has one: to the north-east there's a Moorish fort; no fewer than four ruined fortresses guard the harbour entrance; and two more, still in good repair—the Atalaya and Galeras castles—protect the seafront arsenal, of vital importance to Spain's military.

Immediately west of the Castillo de la Concepción are the ruins of the 13th-century **Iglesia de Santa María Vieja.** Its Romanesque portal is a 19th-century restoration, but the Roman and Byzantine columns, and Roman mosaic floor, are authentic. In the adjacent Calle del Cañón, look for the **well-head** with weathered rope-marks that traditionally inspired Saint Isidore, the youngest of a 6th-century Visigoth duke's four saintly children, to argue the merits of perseverance.

Quite a long trek to the north-west is the small **Museo Arqueológico,** noted for its exceptional collection of Roman mining tools used to extract the considerable mineral wealth of La Unión, a neighbouring inland town. Mines there continue to yield lead, which is exported from Cartagena as it has been for centuries.

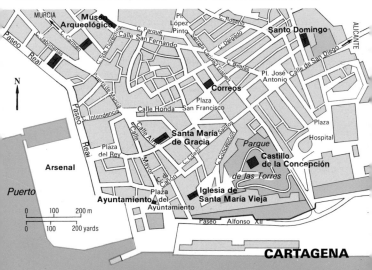

CARTAGENA

Mojácar's cube houses are the jewels of the Sierra Cabrera.

Although the Costa Cálida extending south-west beyond Cartagena has opened up to property development, you can still find quieter stretches of beach. It's a campers' paradise, too, but drinking water can be hard to find away from the main road.

The first stop is **Puerto de Mazarron,** 34 kilometres beyond Cartagena. The spacious beaches here have long been patronized by the Spanish. Now all of Europe has caught on. You'll know **Águilas,** a town of 23,000 people about 50 kilometres farther on, by its 16th-century cas-

tle, which dominates the area. The town offers a wide sandy bay and, to the north, swimming from the rocks around CABO COPE. To the south lie long beaches, excellent for year-round camping.

The N-332 now strikes inland for 32 kilometres to the small town of **Cuevas de Almanzora,** in a hilly region once inhabited by Stone Age man. The numerous caves hereabouts (from which the town takes its name) have been little explored. Most of them are inhabited now by local gypsies.

Follow the N-332 a little farther to VERA, then take the road to **Garrucha** and the coast (the N-340 continues inland until Almeríca). There are six miles of wild, rocky beaches with a dramatic mountain backdrop.

Five kilometres more bring you to thriving **Mojácar**, a village planted on the eastern extremity of the rugged Sierra Cabrera. Purists complain that the cubist effect of steep hillsides dotted with square, flatroofed houses has been spoilt by modern development, but the beaches all around are still pleasant.

About 3,000 years ago, Mojácar was an important Phoenician port, but earthquakes and major geological upheavals have left it high and dry. For centuries the women of Mojácar were kept behind the veil, and the place is still known as the "Village of the Covered Ones". (Interestingly, there's an elegant white statue of a veiled woman outside the church.) Its renown as the "Village of Witches" comes from Mojácar's long and continuing flirtation with faith healing, spells and magic brews. This isolated town is the last bastion of

the mystical sign of the *dalo*, a figure holding a rainbow over his head that was believed to be a talisman against the evil eye. (The word comes from an old Iberian term meaning "Lord of All".) Nowadays, you are more likely to see the *Indalo* in the form of a lucky charm on sale in souvenir shops rather than painted, as it once was, on house doors.

The narrow coastal road continues 22 kilometres more through a moody landscape of barren mountains to CARBONERAS. The long, sandy beaches here are another favourite camping area.

From Carboneras, the road travels 41 kilometres inland through sweeping, treeless moorland to **Níjar**. This developing Andalusian hilltop village is a busy centre for potters, and the narrow streets of the old town centre invite exploration. Look for local ceramics with their characteristic design of tiger stripes and splashes, the colours deliberately allowed to run.

South of Níjar, spectacular cliffs and isolated beaches mark the hard-to-reach natural park of the **Cabo de Gata**. Thanks to a shortage of fresh water, the area has escaped the developers.

The Moorish Legacy Inland

Four historic towns—Elche, Crevillente, Orihuela and Murcia—line the N-340 from Alicante. The most distant of them, Murcia, is only about 80 kilometres away and all four can be visited in a couple of days. While these towns have been influenced by various cultures, the Moorish legacy is predominant in each.

Elche

Thousands upon thousands of date palms overwhelm the eye in Elche, a city as old as the Iberians. The trees, originally planted by the Carthaginians in 300 B.C. or thereabouts, thrive under irrigation. They still stand as the Moors described them, with "feet in water, heads in the fire of heaven". Elche's palms are watered by Abderraman III's 10th-century irrigation system and surround the town of some 200,000 inhabitants on three sides.

Prickly succulents jostle for attention with flowers and date palms in Elche's Hort del Cura.

The **Hort del Cura** (Priest's Grove) is celebrated even in Elche for its cactus, pomegranate and orange trees, and above all, for the *palmera imperial*. This male tree of exceptional age and size has seven branches growing from one main trunk. The *palmera imperial* and many other trees in the grove have been dedicated to royalty and celebrities like Carmen Polo de Franco, the widow of the Generalísimo.

Overlooking the grove's lily-pond is an exact replica of the famous bust of the *Dama de Elche* (The Lady of Elche). The original, dating from 500 B.C. and now housed in Madrid's Archaeological Museum, remains something of a puzzle almost a hundred years after it came to light. If you cover that exotic headdress, you'll see why attributions are difficult to make: the face could be male or female, Spanish, Greek or Eastern.

To visit the place where the bust was discovered go to the nearby hamlet of LA ALCUDIA. Be sure to see the exhibits of Iberian and Roman finds displayed in the excellent local museum. On the way, you'll see palms that look rather like giant asparagus tips. *Encapuchadores* bind these male trees in spring to produce the pale, bleached fronds that are used in Palm Sunday celebrations. These branches, once suitably blessed, are said to conduct lightning, and you'll

---

Royal Palms

Two date palms in the Hort del Cura supply the Spanish royal household with fruit. The specially chosen trees were dedicated to Spain's reigning monarchs, King Juan Carlos and Queen Sophia, during a traditional ceremony which they attended in 1977.

The palms were first watered with wine by the King and Queen. Signs with the names of the monarchs were then hung on the trees by caretakers, who scaled the slippery trunks to cut bunches of dates for the royal couple to sample.

Theirs aren't the only palms with a royal pedigree. The famous *palmera imperial* was dedicated to Empress Elizabeth of Austria during the visit she made to the grove in 1894. Another tree provided Otto of Austria and Hungary with dates. With more than a thousand palms, many of them over 200 years old, the Hort del Cura is a noble sight, even by royal standards.

Nobody knows for sure who the mysterious Dama de Elche represents. The 500 B.C. original is exhibited in Madrid's Archaeological Museum.

see them attached to houses all over Spain. The female palms make a less esoteric annual contribution of 10,000 tons of dates, which ripen in December and are prized for their juicy sweetness.

Back in Elche, there are more palm trees to see and more luxuriant tropical foliage to admire. You can dine and dance in the frond-slatted shade of the **Parque Municipal**, which also features citrus trees and a noisy frog pond. Or visit the **Hort de Baix** and the **Hort del Chocolater** (the latter open at irregular intervals)—these groves help make Elche one of the most verdant cities in Europe.

Not far from the Municipal Park, the **Calahorra, Tower**, "Guardian of Elche", once formed part of the main gate in the long-vanished wall that surrounded Elche in Moorish times.

Next to the tower you'll see the blue dome of the Iglesia de Santa María. The church was **61**

built in the 17th century and rebuilt after being damaged during the Civil War. Every August a spectacular form of sacred theatre, *El Misterio de Elche (The Mystery of Elche)*, is performed here by an amateur cast of priests, civic dignitaries and other local people. The play has been presented in Elche for more than five centuries. The music, Gregorian and traditional, is sung in old *lemosín*. However, the story it tells of the Assumption of the Virgin is quite easily understood.

Across the main road from the church you can't miss the solid **Alcázar de la Señoría**, known locally as the Palacio de los Altamira, with its square towers. This Moorish palace formed part of the city wall. In times past, Spanish monarchs such as James the Conqueror and Ferdinand and Isabella stayed here.

The Vinalopó River, spanned by a bridge here, supplies the water that is still carried to the *horts* in canals dug by the Moors.

A short distance from the palace toward the city centre, you come upon the **Ayuntamiento** (Town Hall), with its fine Renaissance façade and Gothic door. Stand back for a good look at the 14th-century Torre del Concejo, a former watch tower. The quaint carved figures of Calendura and Calendureta ring the hours and quarter hours, as they have done since 1759.

Crevillente

Nineteenth-century travellers sped through neighbouring Crevillente in fear of the notorious bandit James the Bearded. Today, Crevillente's industrial appearance similarly induces haste. But those unattractive factories produce 70 per cent of Spain's handsome woven rugs and carpets, and many invite visitors.

Crevillente was the birthplace of the Arab surgeon Al-Xafra, and during his 13th-century heyday, the town was a good place in which to fall ill. The progressive Moor's treatise on "wounds, inflamations and tumours" may sound hair-raising today, but his treatment of broken bones by padded splints, traction and bitumen casts was actually centuries ahead of its time.

The **Museo Municipal Mariano Benlliure**, alongside the church, contains a collection of works in bronze, marble and clay by the modern sculptor Mariano Benlliure (1868–1947), among them likenesses of the famous men of his day. You'll also see some of his **pasos**—sculpture in life size or larger, a feature of religious processions, particularly during Holy Week.

Orihuela

Situated on the usually peaceful banks of the River Segura, Orihuela is a few kilometres off the busy A-7. Water is drawn from the Segura for the irrigation of the town's extensive groves and fertile fields. When the expulsion of the *moriscos*—once the town's agricultural labourers—threatened the fertility of Orihuela's crops in 1609, brave townspeople hid away enough converted Moors to ensure a good harvest.

The **old university**, on the northern outskirts of the city, was constructed in the 16th and 17th centuries. It's now a school, the Colegio de Santo Domingo (St. Dominic's School). Ask permission to visit the spreading baroque cloisters, magnificent staircase and beautifully tiled refectory. Near the school you'll see all that's left of the town's original wall, the **Puerta de la Olma** (Elm Tree Gate).

A quiet Romanesque cloister adjoins Orihuela's cathedral. She-devil (right) is the picture of evil.

Holiday Inn ®

★★★★

PL. CARLOS TRIAS BERTRAN, 4
ACCESOS POR C/ ORENSE, 22-24
TELEFONO 456 80 00 - FAX 456 80 01
28020 MADRID

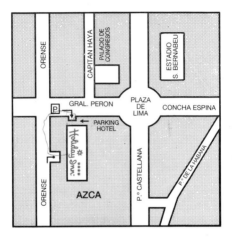

EL HOTEL DISPONE
DE LOS SIGUIENTES SERVICIOS:

- Restaurante LA TERRAZA
- Bar LA CARABELA
- Bar LA TASCA
- Salones para convenciones
- Salones para bodas y banquetes

Now make for the Plaza de Caturla, a small square on the western outskirts of Orihuela. From here you can ascend a hill to the old **Seminario de San Miguel** (Saint Michael's Seminary) which offers panoramic views of Orihuela below and a ruined castle above.

There are many historic buildings to see in Orihuela and the town remains much as it was centuries ago, despite an earthquake in 1829 and present-day industrialization. The Gothic **cathedral**, begun in the early 14th century, with spiral rib vaulting and ornamental grille-work, is considered one of the region's finest.

The **Museo Diocesano de Arte Sacro** (Diocesan Museum of Sacred Art) features a famous painting by Velázquez, called the *Temptation of Saint Thomas Aquinas*.

The fine Romanesque **cloister** was moved here from a nearby convent that suffered damage in the Civil War. It was erected around an early Gothic cross that is Orihuela's austere monument to Spain's war dead.

Orihuela's new **Museo de Semana Santa** (the Easter Week Museum) features the massive floats by Salzillo and other artists, depicting Biblical scenes with life-like statues. A bizarre curiosity here is the *Paso de la Diablesa* (She-Devil Statue). The ghastly horned face of the devil has been terrifying the irreverent into repentance since 1688, when Nicolas de Busi carved it. Every year the she-devil and her companion, a carved skeleton, are trundled through Orihuela as a "warning to the wise".

Murcia

Like Elche and Orihuela, Murcia has been a rich oasis since Moorish times. Its market gardens, second only to Valencia's, are watered by the River Segura and yet another Moorish irrigation system. Today's provincial capital was a favourite city of the Moors and in 1224 they even made it the capital of a small *taifa*, or break-away kingdom.

The most celebrated local hero was the powerful yet benign Cardinal Belluga y Moncada. This warlike prelate thwarted the all-conquering Archduke Charles of Austria in 1707, during the War of the Spanish Succession, preventing Charles from advancing by flooding Murcia's fields, then attacking the invader with a small army recruited at his own expense.

Murcia's cathedral stands on the plaza named in honour of Cardinal Belluga. Construction of the **Catedral de Santa María** (on the site of a mosque) began in 1394. There's not a hint of the 14th century in its splendid western façade, however. This baroque renovation, one of Jaime Bort's celebrated designs, was undertaken when the original Gothic front suffered irreparable damage in a disastrous flood of the Segura in 1735. You can climb the round tower that rises from the north side of the building. There's an impressive view at the top of its five storeys, which are easily ascended.

Inside the cathedral, the Capilla de los Vélez (Chapel of the Vélez) is remarkable for its Plateresque decoration. This highly ornamental style is typical of 16th-century Spain. The *coro* (choir) shelters a *Christ* by Francisco Salzillo, one of many supremely realistic works by this

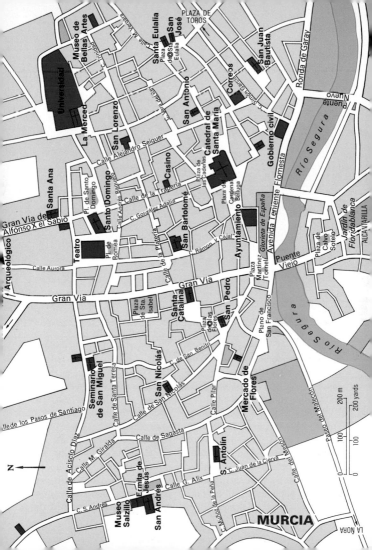

native son of Murcia. Others (a *Saint Jerome* and a *Virgin*) are on display among the chalices and *retablos* of the Museo Diocesano, adjoining the Cathedral.

Before you leave the sanctuary, visit the Capilla Mayor (Main Chapel). The strangest of the cathedral's treasures is contained in an urn here—the heart of Alfonso the Wise, bequeathed to Murcia by the 13th-century king long before his death.

Go out of the cathedral on the north side and walk across Plaza Hernandez Amores to the cool and classy **Calle de la Trapería** (Street of Secondhand Merchants). But don't look for bargains here; the name of this pedestrian thoroughfare belies the elegance of its shops. At the north end you come upon the **Casino** (a private club, not a gambling establishment), with spirited turn-of-the century decor.

*Modern steel waterwheel propelled by old Moorish irrigation system.
Left: the west front of Murcia Cathedral is a tribute to baroque design.*

The entrance hall, an exact copy of the Hall of Ambassadors in Seville's Alcázar, and the ladies' lavatory—with its ceiling of cherubs—are the most magnificent rooms. (Don't forget a small tip to the steward who shows you around.)

During the Casino's heyday, the pedestrian **Calle de la Platería** (Street of Silversmiths), at right angles to the Trapería, was full of practising craftsmen. Flower stalls in the Plaza de las Flores are open every morning. After 11 a.m., vendors tend to retreat into nearby shops and bars, particularly in hot weather.

North-west of the city centre is the Ermita de Jesús church and its impressive **Museo Salzillo**. The highly important group of sculptures gathered here represents every facet of Francisco Salzillo's work. During a career that spanned the 18th-century, Salzillo produced large processional figures still carried in Holy Week celebrations and small, intimate carvings, some of them on a miniature scale.

Waterwheels have been operating in the Murcia region for over a thousand years. You can see one at **La Ñora**, 6 kilometres from the Murcia city centre. The original wheel has been replaced with a steel one, but the Moorish system is otherwise virtually unchanged. A few kilometres farther, in the direction of Granada on the N-340, the **Museo de la Huerta** (Agriculture Museum) at ALCANTARILLA adjoins a second waterwheel, also of steel. Museum exhibits present all aspects of Murcian country life, including traditional furnishings.

At the end of a hard day's sightseeing, nothing can beat a cruise off the Murcia coast. The setting sun is always a glorious spectacle.

What to Do

The Bullfight

Experts swear that it takes a lifetime to learn all the subtleties of the *corrida*, or *fiesta brava*, as the bullfight is known in Spain. But don't let that discourage you. However you may feel about this controversial sport, it remains very much a part of Spanish life,

You'll see the *corrida* at its most thrilling in the demanding rings of Alicante, Cartagena and Murcia. Top matadors—qualified *toreros* who fight fully grown half-ton bulls—occasionally appear in Benidorm, while novice fighters can be seen in other tourist centres. Don't underestimate newcomers to the ring. Among them may be another El Cordobés on the way up.

Perhaps the best seats to buy for a first fight are *sol y sombra, tendido bajo*, lower stands in the sun part of the time and in the shade the other. The first two rows are the most expensive. Admission prices are lower in Alicante than in Benidorm. Tickets everywhere are 20 per cent more than the official price when purchased from agencies and as much as 40 per cent more from hotels. Whether you have booked in advance or not, try to arrive at the *plaza de toros* with an hour to spare, enough time to watch the crowd and feel the tension rising. The *corrida* always starts on time—even if the clock occasionally has to be stopped.

The usual six bulls, fought by three matadors, give an average spectacle of 2½ hours, so a cushion hired on the spot is a good idea. You should remember that the bullfight is neither a sport nor a competition. It's a highly ritualized three-act art form that depends initially on the aggressiveness of the bull and the torero's skill and ability to take risks. No risk, and there would be no bullfight.

Each phase of the fight is closely controlled by the *presidente* from his flag-draped box. He drops two handkerchiefs, one to signal the swaggering parade that precedes the fight and the other to release the first bull from the *puerta de toriles*, the matador's "gate of fear", for the opening act or first *tercio*. The bull is played with magenta capes—first by the matador's team, or *cuadrilla*, then by the matador himself. All the time the *torero* is assessing the bull, noting his temperament, how he charges, how he uses his horns.

The *picador's* moment comes during the second *tercio*, when he rides into the ring on a horse protected by padding. His task is to lance the bull's huge shoulder muscles; it's unattractive but necessary, both to weaken the bull and to lower his head for the kill. Too much lance, and the *picador* ruins the fight. Too little, and he gives the *torero* an impossible task.

Now *banderillas*—long, ribboned, steel-tipped darts—are plunged into the bull's shoulders. In a moment of grace and athleticism, the *banderillero*, or even the matador himself, runs obliquely across the path of the bull, barely pausing as he jack-knifes over the horns to thrust home the darts.

The third and final *tercio* is known as *la suerte de la muerte* or the "act of death". The *torero* steps alone into the ring and plays the bull with the small, red cape or *muleta*—taunting him, calling him, passing those horns within inches of his body. *Olés* and crescendos from the band mean the *matador* is doing well, but if you hear whistles and the cry *¡fuera!* (out!), you'll know he's struggling.

At the moment of highest tension, the *matador* leans over the horns to thrust his sword deep into the bull's aorta for the kill. Success means instant death. But the target, a tiny fist-sized area between the shoulders, can only be reached when the animal's feet are together; and swift kills, which need strength as well as skill and nerve, don't always happen.

If the fight has been good and the kill clean, the *presidente* will award the *torero* one or both of the bull's ears and, for exceptional performances, the tail too. An ear is usually the signal for a lap of honour, and, if the crowd agrees with the award, flowers, and *botas* of wine shower into the ring. Very occasionally an exceptional performance by the bull earns him a reprieve for breeding. In this case, the *presidente* drops a green handkerchief and the crowd goes wild.

The *corrida* is not for everyone—not even for every Spaniard. But see one, preferably several, before you pass judgement on this extraordinary institution.

Folk Dance

The best known traditional dances on the Costa Blanca are the *jota valenciana* and *jota murciana*. Sets of vivacious performers either dance alone facing a partner or in pairs. Their steps can be vigorous or stately and gracious.

The dancers are accompanied by musicians playing the guitar or instruments introduced into the region by the Moors—the *dulzaina* (flute) and *tamboril* (tambourine). The rhythms go all the way back to the Iberians and reflect a diversity of influences, from Moorish to Aragonese and Castilian to Cuban.

Folk dancers start young to perfect their technique. It's not unusual for lively extempore performances to be held in local back streets.

Both old and young take part attesting to the growing revival of interest in Spain's rich heritage of traditional dance and music.

Flamenco

Guitars, the rhythm of castanets and drumming heels, and taut, anguished songs—that's flamenco. You'll be left breathless by these songs and dances from Andalusia.

There are two distinct forms of flamenco: the *cante jondo* (deep song) is an outpouring of intense, soul-searching emotions. The agonized songs, heavy with the wail of Arabia, come from deep within the singer, while the dances are formal and sombre. *Cante jondo* is seldom heard outside Andalusia and Madrid, except on recordings.

Not so the *cante chico* (light song), a more animated version performed in *tablaos* (floor shows) on the Costa Blanca. With a little luck, you may even see flamenco performed by a top Spanish dance company touring on behalf of the Ministry of Information and Tourism's *Festivales de España*. Although the songs may express something of the *cante jondo's* desolation, the dancing is very different. The *fandango*, *tango*, *farruca* and *zambra* are performed to the staccato rhythm of *palmadas* (hand-clapping), *pitos* (finger-snapping), the *zapateado* of fiercely drumming heels and the fiery compulsion of the castanets.

In the *tablaos* and on the stage, the women, their hair swept severely back, swirl flounced and flowing, tight-waisted dresses. The men perform in the Cordoban suit— slightly flared, high-waisted trousers, frilled shirt and short jacket. These traditional costumes and the fervent pride of the performers who wear them make for a colourful spectacle without equal on the cabaret stage.

Festivals

There are so many religious and folk celebrations on the Costa Blanca that you are bound to see one whenever you go. The following list is a selection of major events only. Where dates are movable, check with the Spanish National Tourist Office in your country or, better still, with the local office in Spain.

March or April

Cartagena and nationwide	*Semana Santa* (Holy Week): nationwide week-long Easter celebrations; deeply religious and often lavishly costumed.
Valencia and nationwide (12–19)	*Las Fallas*: Papier maché scenes are made and burnt on the night of the 19th.
Murcia (movable)	*Fiesta de la Primavera* (Spring Festival): folklore and fantasy parades, fireworks and fanfares begin the week following Holy Week.

April

Alcoy (movable)	*Moros y Cristianos* (Moors and Christians): brilliantly costumed parade and sham battle held on or about Saint George's Day.
General, especially Alicante (23)	*Fiesta de San Jorge y Día de Cervantes* (St.George's and Cervantes' Day): book fair and Day of Lovers; animation and colour.
Alicante (movable)	*Semana Mediterránea de la Música* (Classical Music Festival): top performers and orchestras.

June

Alicante (including the 24th)	*Hogueras de San Juan* (Saint John's Eve): a week midsummer festival with parades, fireworks, the bonfires and bullfight.

July

Benidorm	*Festival Español de la Canción* (Song Festival): major Spanish song festival.
Villajoyosa (24–31)	*Moros y Cristianos* (Moors and Christians): the Costa Blanca's most spectacular local historical pageant; see p. 34.
Mar Menor (end July-mid August)	Various regattas.

August–September

Torrevieja	*Festival de Habaneras*; see p. 50.
Elche (13–15 August)	*Misterio de Elche* (Elche mystery play): performed in two parts on 14 and 15 August, preceded by a public dress rehearsal of both parts on 13 August.
Játiva (15–20 August)	*Gran Feria de Játiva*: originally a horse fair dating from 1250; now includes general festivities, especially *Día del Turista* (Tourist's Day).

| Denia and Jávea (movable) | *Moros y Cristianos*: Moors and Christians come in from the sea, and battle ensues, resulting in the Moors being driven back. |
| Bocairent (29 August–2 September) | *Fiesta de Danza Folklórica* (Folkdance Festival) *Día de San Agustín*. |

Boys dressed as soldiers act out one of the most colourful and exciting historical processions in all of Spain—Moros y Cristianos.

Sports and Recreation

Beaches and Swimming

Much of your Costa Blanca holiday will be spent on the beaches—and there are hundreds of miles of them. Some slope gently and are thronged with people; others are tucked away in coves beneath spectacular cliffs assuring all the privacy and tranquillity of a desert island. (see Beaches, BLUEPRINT, p. 104).

Like resorts elsewhere in the Mediterranean, those on the Costa Blanca have no lifeguards. There are Red Cross offices on the most popular beaches. Flags are used at all beaches to advise swimmers of sea conditions: a green flag means the sea is safe for swimming, while a red flag warns of danger. Normal precautions apply here as elsewhere: watch out for water-skiers and speed-boats, which sometimes stray from their flagged areas, and never swim immediately after a meal or long sunbathing.

You can laze in the sun or search for treasure in spectacular undersea caverns just offshore.

Most of the beaches with fine sand are to the north of Alicante. In general, these have been developed as resorts and offer all sorts of facilities—everything from speedboats and parachutes to deck chairs and sunshades. The farther south you go, the fewer provisions you'll find for water-related activities, except at the splendid La Manga resort. The beaches towards the south can be pebbly, while the sand is usually coarse. But the area beyond Cartagena remains largely undiscovered; crowds are rare on this stretch of coast, so if you're not looking for companionship this is the place to enjoy a solitude disturbed only by the crash of waves on the shore.

Away from the beach, there's swimming at Benidorm's Aqualand, a water fun park.

Snorkelling and Scuba Diving

For a new perspective on the wonders of the deep all you need is a mask and breathing tube; the fins are optional. Snorkelling is at its best off cliffs and near rocks. Offshore, snorkellers are required, for safety reasons, to tow a marker buoy.

For more profound sea experiences, try scuba diving. Several centres provide all equipment, a dive boat, expert local knowledge, and sometimes tuition, too. A diving permit is required under Spanish law. Unless you speak reasonable Spanish and know where to go, let your chosen diving centre deal with the documentation.

Diving is virtually always safe: the rips, currents, tides and giant predators of other seas scarcely exist. All cliffs and islands, including Benidorm's small reef, offer interesting diving. Local experts will show you where to find air-locked caves, probe modern wrecks full of surprises, or watch a fresh-water spring bubble mistily from the seabed. The waters around Calpe's Peñón have a tremendous variety of such sealife as the big-mouthed grouper, the rare zebra-striped bream and the Turkish wrasse. Any archaeological finds (and they are rare) must be handed in to the Comandancia de Marina.

Alicantinos *favour nearby Santa Pola beach. There's no better place to meet the local people.*

Boating

Most beaches offer some sort of boat for hire, but the only resorts with a variety of craft to choose from are on the Mar Menor. Benidorm is usually the most expensive resort.

You can take a pedal boat, a stable two-seater propelled by a bicycle-like waterwheel. (Young children should be accompanied.) *Gondolas,* open, banana-shaped boats powered by a double-ended paddle, are not suitable for small children. Although many of the larger beaches have a few assorted sailing boats for hire, La Manga is the place for the keen sailor.

Wind-Surfing

Wind-surfing is the coast's fastest-growing sport, but it's also one of the most difficult. With agility and practice however, and the help of an ocean breeze, you'll soon feel you're flying.

Water-Skiing

Rising fuel costs mean that water-skiing is becoming an expensive sport. All the more reason to double-check rival schools **81** for length of runs, number of attempts allowed for "getting up" and discounts for multiple runs. Serious lessons are usually confined to the early morning, when the sea is calmest. For something less energetic, try powerboat parachuting. You needn't even get your feet wet, and the view is superb.

Water-skier and boat trace the sea with jet-like streams of foam. The sport is fun and easy to learn in the Mediterranean's calm, clear waters.

Fishing

The rivers of the Costa Blanca region may reveal carp and barbel, but don't expect much excitement. The best freshwater fishing hereabouts is the Amadorio Dam, 4 kilometres from Villajoyosa (see p.46) and, to a lesser extent, Guadalest's dam. They hold barbel, the biggest carp, smallish black bass and rainbow trout—introduced in 1977 and still protected. To catch them you'll need a licence with a trout supplement. The season for non-mountain trout runs from the first Sunday in March to August 15. The Ministry of Agriculture and Fisheries oversees licences.

If you go sea fishing, you will need local knowledge to hook big grey mullet, sea bream and bass, maybe even grouper, below quiet cliffs, and mackerel two or three miles out. In summer, you may catch the tasty dorada; in late summer, autumn and winter, various species of tuna and swordfish.

Tennis

A hotel court will probably be your best chance for a game of tennis, but it may not be possible to hire balls and racquets. La Manga has over 30 courts, many of them at hotels. These include 15 at the Golf Club, where there are both clay and grass courts.

Golf

All golf courses on the Costa Blanca are open to visitors, and clubs, caddies and occasionally, electric trolleys can be hired (see p.103). The two 18-hole Kentucky blue-grass courses near La Manga, with their shady palms, are the region's lushest. There is also a fine 18-hole course at Torrevieja's Club Villa Martín and three good 9-hole courses: Altea-la-Vieja's Don Cayo, where hills test legs as well as golfing skills, the San Jaime Club de Ifach between Calpe and Moraira, and the Club de Golf in Jávea.

Riding

For centuries, horse-riding has been a Spanish speciality. One kind of ranch, catering to the resort trade, provides a quiet seaside jog. The other offers good horses, skilled instruction and interesting cross-country riding. For the experienced and saddle fit, there are also mountain treks of up to five days, for instance via Altea's Río Algar or from La Sella, near La Jara. These treks go through orange, almond and olive groves, past gaunt carob trees, across rivers, and up through pine forests and open moors to real Sierra country.

Alternatively, inexperienced riders can join other tourists on horseback for a moonlight excursion, with a barbecue at the end of an easy ride. It's an excellent way of meeting people.

Bird-Watching

Ornithologists, bring your binoculars. The Costa Blanca is crossed by principal migration routes and holds considerable, often unsuspected bird life. In summer, if you sit by any reason-

ably quiet estuary, you may see black tern.

In autumn and winter, bird-watchers search cliffs, particularly Calpe's Peñón, for the rare Audouin's Gull: look out for a small, sleek "herring gull" with dark olive legs and a heavyish red bill, banded in black.

In winter the Salinas de la Mata, just south of Guardamar, often (but not always) attracts thousands of migratory flamingos, a few of which sometimes stay to breed.

Hunting and Shooting

Spain has always been famously rich in hunting and shooting possibilities, from wolf to wild boar—though the Costa Blanca is hardly the place for it. Tourist offices have a brochure, "*Caza*", which tells where to go and how to go about obtaining permits.

Shopping

You will often find the Costa Blanca's best buys off the main streets or in the markets. For the greatest variety and lowest overall prices shop in Alicante and its side-streets. For special items, go inland to the place of manufacture, keeping in mind the prices asked on the coast and at home: Guadalest for ponchos and shawls: Gata for cane, basket work and guitars; Crevillente for woven rugs and carpets: Jijona for *turrón*; Ibi for toys.

If you're motorized, look for good prices at hypermarkets outside the major towns.

Save your bargaining for the gypsies and antique dealers, but remember that they have been at it a long time. Beware of *rebajas* (sales); they may be genuine but reductions are generally few and far between, especially in season.

The Spanish government levies a value-added tax (called IVA) on most items. Tourists from overseas can get a refund on the IVA they've paid on purchases over a stipulated amount. Major tourist shops have forms and details. The refund eventually arrives at your home address.

Summer shopping hours are generally from 10 a.m. to 2 p.m. and from 5 p.m. to 8 p.m. (During the rest of the year shops open later and close earlier.) The big Alicante and Valencia department stores stay open during the traditional siesta, which is the quietest time to shop. In the tourist season, small shops often

Handmade wineskins and pretty shawls are yours for the asking.

stay open on a Saturday evening and Sunday morning.

Bakeries and newsagents open mornings only on most fiestas—but don't count on it.

Best Buys

Antiques can be good buys, but beware of fakes. Look for copper and brass, hand-painted tiles—usually rescued from old houses—and simple oil lamps. If you can find one, and carry it home, buy a traditional cradle. Few are authentically antique, but they are decorative and excellent for holding all sorts of things—even babies.

Cuban cigars are exceptional value for money. Canary Island cigars and locally made cigarettes are even cheaper.

Leather goods are no longer a bargain in Spain, though very good quality products may be priced lower than at home.

Lladró porcelain has long been a collector's item. The Lladró brothers opened their factory in Tabernes Blanques, near Valencia, in 1958. Opposite is a seconds shop with greatly reduced prices. Less detailed models are sold under the name *Nao*.

Mat and basket-work has been a local craft for 1,500 years and is not very expensive.

Ponchos and knitted shawls from Guadalest are colourful and attractive.

Rugs woven in Crevillente are long-wearing and can be made to your own design.

A simple basket or handy bag takes hours of patient weaving.

Souvenirs are tempting purchases: pottery of all shapes, sizes, uses and prices—some featuring Moorish designs; bullfight and flamenco posters with your name topping the bill; low-crowned, broadbrimmed Cordoban leather hats; hand-painted fans; elegant *mantillas* (the traditional lace shawls for special occasions); and *botas*, soft leather wine bottles. (Avoid those with plastic linings.)

Wining and Dining

Far more interesting than the so-called international cuisine, the hearty local dishes are worth seeking out: ingredients come fresh from the sea or the farm and are served with a wide choice of the region's excellent vegetables. Most tourist hotels and restaurants specialize in caution, with menus guaranteed to cause neither rapture nor complaints. Ask around and find out where Spaniards and resident expatriates eat.*

Soups and Stews

The favourite dish of many visitors is the Andalusian "liquid salad", *gazpacho*. This chilled, highly-flavoured soup, to which chopped tomatoes, peppers, cucumbers, onions and croutons are added, is a rousing refresher on a hot summer day. *Caution: gazpachos* with an *s* is quite a different dish (see p. 90).

* For a comprehensive glossary of Spanish wining and dining, ask your bookshop for the Berlitz EUROPEAN MENU READER.

Michirones is a splendid mixture of broad beans, chunks of ham, paprika, sausage and hot peppers, plus tasty bits of this and that. *Pebereta talladeta* started life as a stew composed of potatoes, pepper and tunny fish gills. But today, thick tunny steaks are often the main ingredient. *Guisado de pavo*, turkey stew, is a gastronomic must. To do justice to this speciality of Orihuela, be sure to order it at least six hours in advance.

Rice and Paella

Excellent rice *(arroz)* has grown on the Costa Blanca's doorstep since Moorish times; hence the many rice dishes and, king of them all, world-famous *paella*. *Paella* is named after the large, shallow iron pan in which it is cooked and served. The basis is rice, soaked in stock, coloured yellow with locally grown saffron and fried. *Paella valenciana* adds meat, usually crisply fried chicken and pork, and a seasonal variety of peas, green beans, peppers and other vegetables. *Paella alicantina* is the same, plus generous portions of whole prawns, mussels, small whole crabs, octopus, and slices of lemon. A good one is a gastronomic thrill! **89**

Spaniards only eat *paella* at midday—often, unbelievably, as part of a four-course meal. But, if you want one at midnight, a restaurant will most likely oblige. A good *paella* is always made to order and takes about 30 minutes to prepare.

Fish and Seafood

The seafood and fish of the Mediterranean provide some of the coast's most memorable meals. A great favourite is *zarzuela de mariscos*, a variation of a Catalan dish, which combines many different ingredients, just like the Spanish operetta from which it takes its name. Shellfish is served with rice in an unlikely but very tasty sauce of olive oil, ground almonds, assorted spices and chocolate, though local cooks sometimes cheat a bit by adding octopus and other shell-less titbits.

Then there is *langosta*—spiny lobster—as succulent and as expensive as ever, and sometimes priced per 100 grammes (be sure to read the menu's small print to make sure). *Gambas* are prawns, and *langostinos* the jumbo-sized version. Try them *a la plancha* (grilled), *a la romana* (fried in batter) or *al pil pil* in a hot spicy sauce. *Emperador* (swordfish) is especially good grilled, and *lenguado* (sole) is delicious in batter, grilled, or sautéed in butter. For something different, try *dorada a la sal*: a whole fish is packed in wet salt, then baked. It comes to the table in a shiny white jacket that is broken when the fish is cut and served.

These seafood dishes tend to be rather expensive. But there are some cheaper options. Try *calamares* (squid), for instance; they are marvellous deep-fried (*a la romana*), stuffed (*rellenos*) or cooked in their own ink (*en su tinta*). *Mejillones* (mussels) can be remarkably good steamed with a dash of white wine and garlic. *Caballa*, the rich-fleshed mackerel, is sometimes available *ahumada* (smoked).

Meat Dishes

Rice and fish dishes make up a substantial part of the local diet. However, meat is used in regional cooking, though in nothing like the same range and imaginative presentation.

Among local meat specialities is *gazpachos* (with a final *s* to distinguish it from the chilled soup). This lusty, well-spiced Costa Blanca dish consists of

There's nothing like fish straight from the sea. On the Costa Blanca seafood is plentiful and cheap and there's all the fun of the market.

pork, chicken, rabbit and snails —and perhaps even a partridge or pigeon. It's stewed in a large frying pan and traditionally eaten on a kind of pancake. *Criadillas* are considered a delicacy. More than one tourist-conscious menu bills them as "mountain oysters", but they are in fact bulls' testicles. When it's time for a splurge, try *cabrito asado* (roast kid) or *cochinillo* (roast suckling pig). Both treats are expensive but delicious.

Alioli, a whipped sauce of fresh garlic and olive oil, accompanies many dishes. It's a piquant speciality of the region, and an excellent one.

Dessert and Fruit

Ice cream, fruit, cheese or *flan* (crème caramel) are the most popular desserts. In the summer and early autumn you will be spoiled with an enormous array of fruit. The weekly markets—the best place to buy—are full of strawberries, *nísperos* (a cousin of the lychee), grapes, figs, melons, peaches, apricots, raspberries, pomegranates, grapefruit, lemons, oranges, tangerines, apples and pears, even locally grown bananas, pineapples and dates.

Tapas

A *tapa* is a mouthful of anything that tastes good and fits on a cocktail stick. The variety is enormous: smoked mountain ham, spicy sausages, cheese, olives (some as big as pigeon's eggs), sardines, mushrooms, mussels, squid, octopus, meat balls, fried fish, plus sauces and exotic-looking specialities of the house. The name comes from the practice, sadly almost vanished, of providing a free bite with every drink. The titbit was put on a small plate traditionally used to cover the glass and came to be called a *tapa*, which means lid.

Touring *tapa* bars is great fun, especially in a town's old quarter. It can be expensive, certainly more than the cost of an orthodox meal, but do try to devote at least an evening to it. The code is simple: one helping is called a *porción*; a large serving is a *ración*; half as much, a *media-ración*.

Breakfast

The Spaniards start the day with bread, a simple roll or the traditional *churro*, a kind of elongated fritter made by pouring a batter-like mixture into a cauldron of hot olive oil. The golden-brown result is dusted with sugar, sometimes coated with chocolate sauce, or both.

In deference to foreign habits, full breakfast (*desayuno completo*) is served at most tourist ho-

For local colour at its best, have tapas in a friendly bar.

tels. This usually consists of fruit juice, coffee, rolls, eggs, and perhaps bacon too. Although oranges grow all around you, freshly squeezed juice is hard to find. Try anyway. Ask for *zumo natural de naranja* (freshly pressed orange juice).

Mermelada means any form of jam. Marmalade lovers should ask for *mermelada de naranja*. If you prefer bitter orange, be sure to specify *naranja amarga*.

Restaurants

The Spanish eat late, but in tourist areas you will be served lunch from 1 p.m. and dinner from 8 p.m. Bills tend to include tax and service charge, but it is usual to leave a small tip: more than 5 per cent is generous.

Spanish restaurants are classified and priced by a system of forks, with facilities and length of menu more relevant than the quality of the food. Five forks

In bars like this up and down the coast, you can relax with a pitcher of wine and let the world go by. Watching the passers-by is half the fun.

guarantee real comfort, but the food will not necessarily be better than in a two-or three-fork establishment, just more expensive. A bargain *menú del dia* (menu of the day) is often proposed. There are restaurants specializing in them, offering three good courses, bread, and a jug of very reasonable *vino de la casa* (house wine).

If you are saving up for a special meal, or just economiz-

ing, fill up on traditional *potajes*, thick soups full of vegetables, stock and goodness, in unpretentious restaurants with one fork or none. Spain's golden potato omelette *(tortilla española)* makes another excellent budget meal. To keep costs down, order *vino de la casa* (wine of the house).

Bars and Cafés

Banish the bars and cafés and you'd disconcert the whole of

Spain. These establishments are at the centre of the country's social life, where workers take an early morning drink and businessmen negotiate; where old men play cards and friends meet to watch the world go by from shaded pavement tables. Traditionally, a drink buys a seat for as long as you want to stay. In areas popular with tourists though, you might find the waiter hovering.

Bars are graded from first to third class and charge accordingly; prices always include service, but a small 5 per cent tip is usual. You will pay up to 15 per cent more for service at a table, especially in tourist centres.

Wines and Spirits

Although wines from the north are considered to be Spain's best, the Costa Blanca's *vino* is very drinkable and very reasonably priced. Look for *Monóvar*, *Pinosa* and the lighter, less plentiful *Ricote* (all available in red, rosé or white). Beware of the innocent-looking red *Jumilla*. Its 18 per cent alcohol content can sneak up on you. Same peril with the strong Alicante dessert wine, ten drops of which were long reckoned to be one of nature's surest cures. Although the pre-scribed amount failed to restore France's ageing Louis XIV to health, it might work wonders with a morning-after feeling. Be sure to taste the Costa Blanca's famous *Moscatel* wine. It's perfect with dessert and preserves all the sweet, distinctive flavour of a Muscat grape.

Try to visit a *bodega*, one of the large wine cellars to be found in towns and most villages. Wine matured in the enormous, dark barrels that line the walls of the older *bodegas* is not much more expensive than *vino corriente* (ordinary wine) from a modern, million-litre vat. Sample before buying, especially the cheaper wines. They cost less than some mineral waters and will be blended to your taste; containers are extra. Sherry (*jerez*), a wine fortified with brandy, has been made in Spain for hundreds of years. By the early 18th century Spain was already exporting it to France. It's hardly surprising, then, that only Spanish sherry can carry the name unlinked with a country of origin. You will find all the world-famous names on the Costa Blanca, all at reasonable prices. If you are baffled by the choice, remember the main types and experiment.

Finos are dry and pale, with a rich bouquet. They are usually taken as aperitifs, particularly *manzanillas*, the driest of all, and *amontillados*. *Olorosos* (which include the brown and cream varieties) are sweet, heavy and dark, and go well with dessert. Somewhere between the two are the *amorosos*. These are medium dry, light amber in colour, and can be ordered for an aperitif or as a dessert wine. Most can be bought from the barrel, blended to your own taste.

Spanish champagne *(Cava)* is mass-produced and reasonably priced but almost always sweet. For a dry drink, look for the description *brut*. Seco (dry) never really is, and *dulce* is very sweet.

There are other sparkling wines, *vinos espumosos*, which, slightly chilled, go down well on a hot day. Spanish brandy is a bit heavy and sweet and bears little resemblance to the best French cognacs. But it is a good, reasonably priced drink. The more expensive varieties are smoother.

Liqueurs abound. Many famous foreign brands (especially French) are made under licence and sell at prices way below those in their home countries. A glance along the shelves of any

Picking grapes is hard work but has good rewards.

bar shows the vast range of Spanish liqueurs. They are mostly sweet and often herbal. Try Alicante's *Cantueso*, made since 1867 and still unknown outside the province.

You'll enjoy *sangría*, an iced, hot-weather drink that combines red wine, brandy and mineral water, with fruit juice, sliced oranges and other fruit and sugar to taste. *Beware*: it can pack a punch, especially when laced with rough brandy, but you can always dilute *sangría* with soda water and plenty of ice.

Other Drinks

Some tourist cafés advertise "tea like mother makes", but in native Spanish establishments, tea is unlikely to evoke dreams of home. Coffee is very good. Learn the coffee code: *café con leche*, similar to French morning coffee, is half coffee, half milk; *café cortado* is strong and served with a dash of cream (or milk); *café solo* is strong and black. Milder, instant coffees are often available. Coffee without caffeine is *descafeinado*.

1 *Manchego cheese* (queso manchego); 2 *Rioja wine* (vino de Rioja); 3 *Sherry* (vino de Jerez); 4 *prawns* (gambas); 5 *sardines* (sardinas); 6 *squid* (calamares); 7 *whitebait* (chanquetes); 8 *grapes* (uvas); 9 *clam* (almeja); 10 *sea bream* (besugo); 11 *green peppers* (pimientos); 12 *Spanish omelette* (tortilla española); 13 *salad* (ensalada); 14 *chilled vegetable soup* (gazpacho).

To Help You Order...

Could we have a table?	**¿Nos puede dar una mesa?**
Do you have a set menu?	**¿Tiene un menú del día?**
I'd like a/an/some...	**Quisiera...**

beer	**una cerveza**	milk	**leche**
bread	**pan**	mineral water	**agua mineral**
coffee	**un café**	napkin	**una servilleta**
cutlery	**los cubiertos**	potatoes	**patatas**
dessert	**un postre**	rice	**arroz**
fish	**pescado**	salad	**una ensalada**
fruit	**fruta**	sandwich	**un bocadillo**
glass	**un vaso**	sugar	**azúcar**
ice-cream	**un helado**	tea	**un té**
meat	**carne**	(iced) water	**agua (fresca)**
menu	**la carta**	wine	**vino**

...and Read the Menu

aceitunas	olives	**langosta**	spiny lobster
albóndigas	meat balls	**langostino**	large prawn
almejas	baby clams	**lomo**	loin
atún	tunny (tuna)	**mariscos**	shellfish
bacalao	codfish	**mejillones**	mussels
besugo	sea bream	**melocotón**	peach
boquerones	fresh anchovies	**merluza**	hake
calamares	squid	**ostras**	oysters
callos	tripe	**pastel**	cake
cangrejo	crab	**pimiento**	green pepper
caracoles	snails	**pollo**	chicken
cerdo	pork	**pulpitos**	baby octopus
champiñones	mushrooms	**queso**	cheese
chorizo	a spicy pork sausage	**salchichón**	salami
		salmonete	red mullet
chuleta	chops	**salsa**	sauce
cocido	stew	**ternera**	veal
cordero	lamb	**tortilla**	omelette
entremeses	hors-d'oeuvre	**trucha**	trout
gambas	prawns	**uvas**	grapes
jamón	ham	**verduras**	vegetables

BLUEPRINT for a Perfect Trip

How to Get There

If you're planning a trip to the Costa Blanca, you should get in touch with a reliable travel agent who has up-to-date information on fares, special tickets and accomodation.

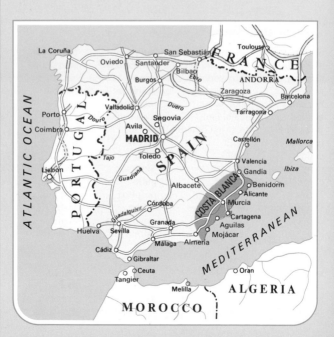

BY AIR

Scheduled flights

The Costa Blanca is served by Alicante and Valencia airports, which are linked by regular flights from several European cities. However, the main gateway to Spain is Madrid's Barajas airport, which is on several intercontinental routes, mainly from North and South America, and Africa; it is also linked frequently to most European and North African cities.

Charter flights and package tours

From the U.K. and Ireland: There are charter flights available to the Costa Blanca, generally as part of package tours. It is possible to find your own accommodation and submit this to your travel agent who can then arrange a "package" with charter flight. Or travel on a charter and use wanderer vouchers to stay in youth hostels, small hotels and the like.

From North America: Barcelona is featured on some Iberian or European packages that let you visit several Spanish cities during a specified period of time. From there, it's possible to hire a car or take the train or bus to Alicante, Murcia and Almería.

From Australia and New Zealand: There are no package tours to any specific Spanish destinations, but independent arrangements may be made.

BY ROAD

The main access road from France to the Costa Blanca is at the eastern side of the Pyrenees via Barcelona on the motorway (expressway) or the more scenic coastal road. You could also travel via Toulouse and cross the Spanish border at Puigcerdá near Andorra and from there travel on the N-152 to Barcelona, or go via Pau (France) to Candanchú and Saragossa or Lleida. There is a long-distance car-ferry service from Plymouth to Santander in northern Spain (a 24-hour trip); from Santander, you can go via Bilbao and follow the A68 and A2 motorways all the way to the eastern coast.

BY RAIL

The *Barcelona-Talgo* links Paris with Barcelona in about 11½ hours. For most other connections you'll have to change trains at Portbou.

Visitors from abroad can buy the *RENFE (Red Nacional de los Ferrocarriles Española*, the Spanish National Railways) *Tourist Card* for a reasonable price, valid for unlimited rail travel within the country for periods of 8, 15 or 22 days (1st and 2nd classes available).

The *Rail Europ S* (senior) card, obtainable before departure only, entitles senior citizens to purchase train tickets for European destinations at reduced prices.

Anyone under 26 years of age can purchase an *Inter-Rail* card which allows one month's unlimited 2nd-class travel in 26 European countries, including Spain. A zonal Inter-Rail card is also now available, valid for 15 days travel in Spain, Portugal and Morocco. The *Freedom Pass* is valid for 3, 5 or 10 days rail travel in any month, in Spain and/or any one or more of 26 European countries.

People living outside Europe and North Africa can purchase a *Eurailpass* for unlimited rail travel in 16 European countries including Spain. This pass must be obtained before leaving home.

When to Go

Obviously summer is the high season on Spain's sunny coasts; this is often the only time the whole family can get away. But if you can plan your trip just before or just after the school holidays you'll find that prices are lower and accommodation easier to find.

The following charts indicate monthly average temperatures in Alicante. Minimum averages were taken at dawn, maximum averages at midday.

		J	F	M	A	M	J	J	A	S	O	N	D
°C	max.	16	17	20	22	26	29	32	32	30	25	21	17
	min.	7	6	8	10	13	15	19	20	18	15	10	7
°F	max.	61	63	68	72	78	84	90	90	86	77	70	63
	min.	45	43	47	50	56	61	66	68	65	59	50	45

Planning Your Budget

To give you an idea of what to expect, here are some average prices in Spanish pesetas (ptas.). However, they must be regarded as *approximate*, as prices vary from place to place, and inflation creeps relentlessly up. Prices quoted may be subject to a VAT tax (IVA) of 4, 7 or 16%.

Airport transfer. Bus from El Altet to Alicante 125 ptas., taxi to Alicante about 1,500 ptas., to Benidorm 6,000 ptas.

Camping (per day). *De luxe* (from): adult 600 ptas., child 500 ptas., car 600 ptas., tent 600 ptas., caravan (trailer) or mobile home 600–1000 ptas., scooter 500 ptas. *Economy:* adult 480 ptas., child 380 ptas., car 480 ptas., tent 480 ptas., caravan 600 ptas., scooter 380 ptas. Add 7% tax.

Car hire (international company). Unlimited mileage including tax and insurance: *Corsa* 24,692 ptas. per week. *Renault 19* 32,833 ptas per week.

Entertainment. Bullfight from 3,000 ptas., cinema 500 ptas., flamenco nightclub (including drink) from 3,000 ptas., disco from 1,000 ptas.

Hairdressers. *Woman's* haircut, shampoo and set or blow-dry 1,400 ptas. *Man's* haircut from 1,000 ptas.

Hotels (double room with bath). ***** 17,700 ptas., **** 16,000 ptas., *** 9,000 ptas., ** 5,500 ptas., * 4,500 ptas. Add 6% tax.

Meals and drinks. Continental breakfast from 450 ptas., *plato del día* 700–750 ptas., meal in good establishment from 2,200 ptas., small beer 125–150 ptas. (in a nightclub/disco from 400 ptas)., coffee 125–150 ptas., Spanish brandy 250 ptas., soft drinks 150 ptas.

Shopping bag. Stick of white bread 70 ptas. (brown from 80 ptas.), 250 grams of butter 275 ptas., dozen eggs 200 ptas., 1 kilo of steak 1,300–1,900 ptas., 250 grams of coffee 280 ptas., 100 grams of instant coffee 435 ptas., 1 litre of fruit juice 89–150 ptas., bottle of wine from 170 ptas.

Sports. *Golf* (per day) green fee from 4,250 ptas. *Tennis* court fee 700 ptas. per hour, instruction from 1200 ptas. per hour. *Windsurfing* from 1,500 ptas. per hour. *Horseback riding* from 2,000 ptas. per hour.

Taxi. Meters start at 500 ptas. Prices for long distance journeys are usually fixed, so check before starting your journey.

An A-Z Summary of Practical Information and Facts

A star (*) following an entry indicates that relevant prices are to be found on page 103. Listed after some basic entries is the appropriate Spanish translation, usually in the singular, plus a number of phrases that should help you seeking assistance.

A **AIRPORT*** *(aeropuerto)*. Alicante Airport, El Altet, handles domestic and international flights. The airport terminal has a restaurant, snack bars, information desks, a currency exchange office, car hire counters, a duty-free shop and a post office (open between 9 a.m. and 2 p.m.).

The porters' rate is written on a tag on their jacket lapels. Taxis are available, or use the airport bus service (6.30 a.m.–9.30 p.m.) 125 ptas.

Where's the bus for …?	**¿De dónde sale el autobús para …?**
What time does the bus leave for …?	**¿A qué hora sale el autobús para …?**
Porter!	**¡Mozo!**

B **BEACHES**

The Alicante Area

Postiguet: about a mile of soft sand; good sports facilities; promenade and cafés alongside.

Albufereta: 150 yards of fine sand; excellent sports facilities; holiday apartments, cafés and bars.

San Juan/Muchavista: several miles of fine sand; good sports facilities; gardens, car park, restaurants and bars nearby.

Towards the North

Campello: half a mile of shingle, pebbles and sand with rocky promontories; promenade restaurants and bars.

Poniente (Benidorm): nearly two miles of fine sand adjoining the old town; good sports facilities; a few cafés.

Levante (Benidorm): over a mile of fine sand; restaurants and hotels nearby; good sports facilities.

Albir: about one mile of pebbly beach; villas, bars and cafés nearby; very good sports facilities.

Olla de Altea: 500 yards of pebbly beach; big hotel; port with marina; sports facilities.

Puerto (Calpe): 150 yards of fine sand with some pebbles; beautiful views of Peñón de Ifach; few sports facilities.

Fosa or Levante (Calpe): nearly a mile of fine sand; park nearby; excellent sports facilities.

Fustera (Calpe): some 50 yards of beach between rocks; some seaweed; no sports facilities.

Castillo (Moraira): 100 yards of fine sand between rocky promontories, ruins of castle nearby; fair provision for sports; port with marina; bars and restaurants nearby.

Portet (Moraira): small beach of shingle and pebbles; mooring for boats; good sports facilities; bars and restaurants nearby.

Granadella (Jávea): small beach of pebbles and fine sand in sheltered bay; no sports facilities; restaurant nearby.

Arenal (Jávea): half a mile of fine sand in bay; excellent sports facilities; restaurants and gardens nearby.

Jávea: 500 yards of pebbly beach at the port; no sports facilities; bar.

Las Marinas (Denia): several miles of sand; excellent sports facilities; bars and restaurants nearby.

Vergel: miles of fine sand; bars and restaurants; no sports facilities.

Playa de Oliva: lovely sandy beach which merges into Playa de Piles; bars and restaurants nearby; some sports facilities.

Gandía: several miles of sandy beach; very well kept; bars, restaurants and good sports facilities.

South of Alicante

Los Arenales del Sol: miles of fine sand; limited sports facilities.

Santa Pola: about 500 yards of fine, grey, pebbly sand; some sports facilities; good restaurants near beach.

Pinet: one mile of fine sand; no sports facilities; restaurant and bar.

Guardamar: several miles of fine sand; very limited sports facilities; amusement arcade; restaurant and bar.

Los Locos (Torrevieja): small beach with coarse sand; bars nearby.

B   *El Cura* (Torrevieja): 500 yards of fine sand; some sports facilities.

Campoamor: 400 yards of soft white sand; good provision for sports; some villas in nearby hills.

La Zenia: small beach with soft sand and rocky promontories; bar and club; no sports facilities.

La Manga: several miles of sandy beaches; fine sand on lagoon; superior provision for sports.

Puerto de Mazarrón: fine sand and pebbles in bays; rocky promontories; villas nearby; good sports facilities.

Aguilas: several sandy beaches; sports facilities.

Mojácar: 500 yards of sand and pebbles; sports facilities; some beach bars; increasingly popular.

C   **CAMPING*** *(camping)*. There are official campsites along the whole of the coast. Facilities vary, but most have electricity and running water. Some have shops, small playgrounds for children, restaurants, swimming pools and even launderettes. For a complete list of campsites, consult any Spanish National Tourist Office (see TOURIST INFORMATION OFFICES).

May we camp here?	**¿Podemos acampar aquí?**
We have a tent/caravan (trailer).	**Tenemos una tienda de camping/una caravana.**

CAR HIRE* *(coches de alquiler)*. There are car hire firms in most resorts and main towns. Rates vary, so check before committing your money. You are legally required to have an International Driving Licence.

A deposit, as well as an advance payment of the estimated rental charge, is generally required, although holders of major credit cards are normally exempt from this. There's a VAT or sales tax (IVA) levied on the total rental charges. When hiring a car, ask for any available seasonal deals.

I'd like to rent a car (tomorrow).	**Quisiera alquilar un coche (para mañana).**
for one day/a week	**por un día/una semana**
Please include full insurance coverage.	**Haga el favor de incluir el seguro a todo riesgo.**

106

CHILDREN. Following are some suggestions for outings with the children, which parents might enjoy too:

Acualand, Benidorm's popular water theme park, features water slides and swimming pools. Closed during the winter months.

Safari Park Vergel is situated about 100 kilometres from Alicante on the inland road from Vergel to Pego. You'll see many species of animals—even dolphins (in the park's dolphinarium). For children there is mini motocross, aquatic scooters, horses, ponies, jumping beds, go-carts, etc.

To find a suitable baby-sitter, make enquiries at your hotel reception desk. Very few hotels have resident sitters, but most of them will engage one for you. Tourists on a package holiday can make arrangements for baby-sitting at their travel agency.

Can you get me a baby-sitter for tonight?	**¿Puede conseguirme una canguro para cuidar los niños esta noche?**

CIGARETTES, CIGARS, TOBACCO (*cigarrillos, puros, tabaco*). Spanish cigarettes can be made of strong, black tobacco (*negro*) or light tobacco (*rubio*). Imported foreign brands are up to three times the price of local makes, though foreign brands produced in Spain under licence can be cheaper than when bought at home. Locally made cigars are cheap and reasonably good. Canary Island cigars are excellent and Cuban cigars are readily available. Pipe smokers find the local tobacco somewhat rough.

Refrain from smoking wherever you see the no-smoking sign. It is now against the law to light up in many public places.

A packet of …/A box of matches, please.	**Un paquete de …/Una caja de cerillas, por favor.**

CLOTHING. Whatever you wear for hot north European summers will be fine for the Costa Blanca. Have a jersey handy in the evenings. Between November and March it can be extremely cold, sometimes with winds, so always carry a jacket or something warm. Even in August be sure to take jerseys when going to the mountains. When visiting churches women no longer *have* to cover their heads, but decent dress is certainly expected.

C **COMMUNICATIONS.** Post offices *(correos)* are for mail, telegrams and faxes (ratesheet available for sending and receiving); normally you can't make telephone calls from them.

Post office hours: 9 a.m. to 1 or 2 p.m. and 4 or 5 to 6 or 7 p.m., Monday to Friday (but some only open in the morning from 9 a.m. to 2 p.m.). Mornings only on Saturday.

Mail: If you don't know in advance where you'll be staying, you can have your mail addressed to the *Lista de Correos* (poste restante or general delivery) in the nearest town. Take your passport along as identification and be prepared to pay a small fee for each letter received. Some post offices limit acceptance of registered mail to certain times. See posted hours.

Postage stamps are also on sale at tobacconists *(tabacos)* and often at hotel desks. Mailboxes are yellow and red.

Telegrams *(telegrama)*: Telegram and post office counter services work independent hours and usually overlap. Times vary from town to town, too, but you can always send telegrams by phone.

You can phone a telegram 24 hours a day, weekends and holidays, from anywhere in Alicante province by calling 5142001. If you are staying at a hotel, the receptionist can take telegrams.

Telephone *(teléfono)*: You can make local and international calls from public telephone booths in the street, from most hotels (often with heavy surcharges) and from some post offices. For international direct dialling, pick up the receiver, wait for the dial tone, then dial 07, wait for a second sound and dial the country code (U.K. 44, Canada/U.S.A. 1), city code (without the initial 0 for the U.K.) and subscriber's number.

To reverse the charges, ask for *cobro revertido*. For a personal (person-to-person) call, specify *persona a persona*.

Can you get me this number in …?	**¿Puede comunicarme con este número en …?**
Have you received any mail for …?	**¿Ha recibido correo para …?**
A stamp for this letter/postcard, please.	**Por favor, un sello para esta carta/tarjeta.**
express (special delivery)	**urgente**
airmail	**vía aérea**
registered	**certificado**

COMPLAINTS. By law, all hotels and restaurants must have official complaint forms *(Hoja Oficial de Reclamación)* and produce them on demand. The original of this triplicate document should be sent to the regional office of the Ministry of Tourism, one copy remains with the establishment complained against, and you keep the third sheet.

In the rare event of major obstruction, when it is not possible to call in the police, write directly to the Secretaría de Estado de Turismo, Sección de Inspección y Reclamaciones, Maria de Molina 50, 28006 Madrid.

New legislation greatly strengthens the consumer's hand. Public information offices are being set up, controls carried out, and fallacious information made punishable by law. For a tourist's needs, however, the tourist office (the *Oficina municipal de Información al Consumidor*) or, in really serious cases, the police, would normally be able to give advice.

CONSULATES *(consulado)*. If you get into serious trouble, seek out the British consulate (see below) which helps citizens of all English-speaking countries (Australia, Eire, New Zealand, South Africa and U.S.A.). The consulate is open from 8.30 a.m. to 2.30 p.m., Mondays to Fridays, 8.30 a.m. to 2.00 p.m. in summer. For exteme emergencies outside office hours, call (tel. 521 60 22) or the Guardia Civil in Alicante (tel. 062).

British Consulate, Plaza de Calvo Sotelo 1–2, Alicante; tel. 521 60 22.

CONVERTER CHARTS. For fluid and distance measures, see page 112. Spain uses the metric system.

Temperature

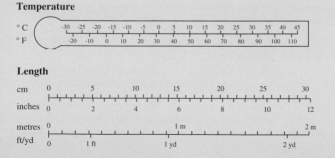

Length

C Weight

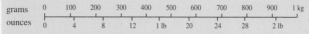

grams	0	100	200	300	400	500	600	700	800	900	1 kg
ounces	0	4	8	12	1 lb	20	24	28	2 lb		

CRIME and THEFT. Spain's crime rate has caught up with the rest of the world. Thefts and break-ins are increasing. Hang on to purses and wallets, especially in busy places—the bullfight, open air markets, fiestas. Don't take valuables to the beach. Lock cars and *never* leave cases, cameras, etc., on view. If you suffer a theft or break-in, report it to the Guardia Civil.

My ticket/wallet/passport has been stolen.	**Me han robado mi billete/ cartera/pasaporte.**

D DRIVING IN SPAIN

Entering Spain: To bring your car into Spain you should have:

International Driving Permit, or a legalized and certified translation of your home licence	Car registration papers	Green Card (an extension to your regular insurance policy, making it valid for foreign countries)

Also recommended: With your certificate of insurance, you should carry a bail bond. If you injure somebody in an accident in Spain, you can be imprisoned while the accident is under investigation. This bond will bail you out. Apply to your automobile association or insurance company.

A nationality sticker must be prominently displayed on the back of your car. Seat belts are compulsory, as are crash helmets for scooters or motor-bikes. Not using them outside towns makes you liable to a stiff fine.

Driving conditions: Drive on the right. Pass on the left. Yield right of way to all traffic coming from the right, and when entering a roundabout, to traffic already on it. Spanish drivers tend to use their horn when passing other vehicles.

Main roads are adequate to very good and improving all the time. Secondary roads can be bumpy. The main danger of driving in Spain comes from impatience, especially on busy roads. A large percentage of accidents in Spain occur when passing, so take it easy. Spanish truck and lorry drivers will often wave you on (by hand signal or by flashing their right directional signal) if it's clear ahead.

Remember that the villages aren't designed for cars, and the older people are still not quite used to them. Drive with extra care to avoid children darting out, and older folk in the middle of the road.

Speed limits: 120 k.p.h. (75 m.p.h.) on motorways (expressways), 100 k.p.h. (62 m.p.h.) or 90 k.p.h. (56 m.p.h.) on other roads, 50 k.p.h. (31 m.p.h.) in towns and built-up areas.

Traffic Police: The armed Civil Guard *(Guardia Civil)* patrols the highways on powerful black motorcycles. Always in pairs, these capable looking characters are courteous, good mechanics and will stop to help anyone in trouble. They are severe on lawbreakers.

If fined, you may be expected to pay on the spot. The most frequent offences include passing without flashing directional-indicator lights, travelling too close to the car ahead and driving with a burnt-out head or tail light. (Spanish law requires you to carry a set of spare bulbs at all times.)

Parking: Most towns have zones in which you may only park during working hours *(horas laborables)* if you have a parking ticket, properly punched. Tickets are sold at tobacconists. Otherwise, there are ticket machines.

Fuel and oil: Fuel is available in super (97 octane), leadfree *(sin plomo—* 95 octane), normal (92 octane) and diesel—but not every petrol station carries the full range outside cities.

Fluid measures

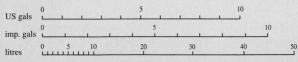

D **Distances:** Here are approximate road distances in kilometres between some provincial and regional centres:

Alicante–Albacete	165	Benidorm–Altea	10
Alicante–Barcelona	520	Benidorm–Cabo de San Antonio	55
Alicante–Benidorm	45	Benidorm–Cabo La Nao	65
Alicante–Elche	25	Benidorm–Calpe	20
Alicante–Gibraltar	665	Benidorm–Denia	60
Alicante–Málaga	520	Benidorm–Jávea	50
Alicante–Murcia	80	Benidorm–Moraira	35
Alicante–Valencia	180	Benidorm–Villajoyosa	10

To convert kilometres to miles:

Distance

km	0	1	2	3	4	5	6	8	10	12	14	16
miles	0	½	1	1½	2	3	4	5	6	7	8	9	10

Breakdowns: Spanish garages are as efficient as any, and a breakdown will probably be cheaper to repair in Spain than in your home country. Spare parts are readily available for Spanish-built cars—Seat, Renault, Simca, Dodge, Citroën, Morris and Austin Minis and 1100s. But spares for other makes may be hard to obtain. Make sure your car is in top shape before leaving home.

Road signs: Most road signs are the standard pictographs used throughout Europe. However, you may encounter these written signs:

¡Stop/Alto!	Stop!
Aparcamiento	Parking
Autopista (de peaje)	(Toll) motorway (expressway)
Ceda el paso	Give way (Yield)
Cruce peligroso	Dangerous crossroads
Cuidado	Caution
Despacio	Slow
Desviación	Diversion (Detour)
Peligro	Danger
Prohibido adelantar	No overtaking (passing)
Prohibido aparcar	No parking
112 Puesto de socorro	First-aid post

(International) Driving Licence	**Carné de conducir (internacional)**
Car registration papers	**Permiso de circulación**
Green Card	**Carta verde**
Full tank, please …	**Llénelo, por favor …**
super/normal	**super/normal**
lead-free/diesel	**sin plomo/diesel**
Check the oil/tires/battery.	**Por favor, controle el aceite/los neumáticos/la batería.**
I've had a breakdown.	**Mi coche se ha estropeado.**
There's been an accident.	**Ha habido un accidente.**

ELECTRIC CURRENT *(corriente eléctrica)*. Today 220-volt A.C. is becoming standard, but older installations of 125 volts can still be found. Check before plugging in. If the voltage is 125, American appliances (e.g. razors) built for 60 cycles will run on 50-cycle European current, but more slowly.

If you have trouble with any of your appliances ask your hotel receptionist to recommend an *electricista*.

| What's the voltage—125 or 220? | **¿Cuál es el voltaje—ciento veinticinco (125) o doscientos veinte (220)?** |
| an adaptor/a battery | **un adaptador/una pila** |

EMERGENCIES. If you're not staying at a hotel, ring or visit the Municipal Police (091) or the Guardia Civil. If possible take a Spanish speaker with you, although some police stations now have interpreters in tourist areas. Depending on the nature of the emergency, refer to the separate entries in this book, such as CONSULATES, MEDICAL CARE, POLICE, etc.

Though we hope you'll never need them, here are a few key words you might like to learn in advance:

Careful	**Cuidado**	Fire	**Fuego**
Help	**Socorro**	Police	**Policía**
Stop	**Deténgase**	Stop thief	**Al ladrón**

E **ENTRY and CUSTOMS FORMALITIES** *(aduana)*. Most visitors require only a valid passport to visit Spain, but Australian, Canadian and New Zealand citizens should apply for a visa. British citizens may no longer enter Spain on a Visitor's Passport; a full passport is required. Though residents of Europe and North America aren't subject to any health requirements, visitors from further afield should check with a travel agent before departure in case inoculation certificates are called for.

The following chart shows customs allowances for certain items of personal use.

Into:	Cigarettes		Cigars		Tobacco	Spirits		Wine
Spain 1)	200	or	50	or	250 g.	1 l.	or	2 l.
Australia	200	or	250 g.	or	250 g.	1 l.	or	1 l.
Canada	200	and	50	and	900 g.	1.1 l.	or	1.1 l.
N.Zealand	200	or	50	or	250 g.	1.1 l.	and	4.5 l.
S.Africa	400	and	50	and	250 g.	1 l.	and	2 l.
U.S.A.	200	and	100	and	2)	1 l.	or	1 l.
Within the EU 3)	800	and	200	and	1kg	10 l.	and	90 l.

1) Arriving from non-EU countries, or EU countries with duty-free.
2) A reasonable quantity.
3) Guidelines for non duty-free within the EU. For the import of larger amounts you must be able to prove that the goods are for your own personal use. For EU duty-free allowances see 1) above.

Currency restrictions: Visitors may bring an unlimited amount of foreign currency into Spain. The amount of spanish currency brought in or taken out of the country is restricted to 1,000,000 ptas. If you intend to bring in and take out again larger sums, declare this on arrival and departure.

I've nothing to declare.   **No tengo nada que declarar.**
It's for my personal use.   **Es para mi uso personal.**

G **GUIDES** *(guía)*. There is no official agency for guides at the moment. Guides are usually attached to local travel agencies and normally accompany their excursions. Free-lancers exist, but agree on a price in advance.

We'd like an English-speaking guide.	**Queremos un guía que hable inglés.**	**G**
I need an English interpreter.	**Necesito un intérprete de Inglés.**	

HAIRDRESSERS'* *(barberia; peluqueria)*. Most large hotels have their **H** own salons and the standard is generally very good. It is necessary to telephone for an appointment at women's hairdressers'. Salons are open six days a week, from 9 a.m. to 1 p.m. and 4.30 to 9 p.m. in summer and 9 a.m. to 1 p.m. and 3.30 to 7.30 or 8 p.m. in winter. Salons open only from 9 a.m. to 1 p.m. on Saturday in winter.

Not too much off (here).	**No corte mucho (aquí).**
A little more off (here).	**Un poco más (aquí).**
haircut	**corte**
shampoo and set	**lavado y marcado**
blow-dry	**secar a mano**
permanent wave	**permanente**
a colour rinse/hair-dye	**champú colorante/tinte**
a colour chart	**un muestrario**

HITCH-HIKING *(auto-stop)*. In Spain, hitch-hiking is strictly forbidden on Motorways and toll roads. If you sleep out in the open, don't bed down close to camping and caravan (trailer) sites. Police passing the campsite may awaken you to check your identity.

Can you give us a lift to …?	**¿Puede llevarnos a …?**

HOTELS and ACCOMMODATION* *(hotel; alojamiento)*. Spanish hotel prices are no longer government-controlled. Before the guest takes a room he fills out a form with hotel category, room number and price and signs it. Breakfast is generally included in the room rate.

When you check into your hotel you might have to leave your passport at the desk. Don't worry, you'll get it back in the morning.

H **Other accommodation:**

Hostal and **Hotel-Residencia:** Modest hotels, often family concerns, also graded by stars.
Pensión: Boarding house, few amenities.
Fonda: Village inn, clean and unpretentious.
Parador: State-run establishment usually located outside of towns. Advance booking essential in season.

I'd like a single/double room.	**Quisiera una habitación sencilla/doble.**
with bath/shower	**con baño/ducha**
What's the rate per night?	**¿Cuál es el precio por noche?**

L **LANGUAGE.** Nobody appreciates efforts to learn their language more than the Spanish, and a few words go a long way. *Castellano* (Castilian), Spain's official language, is understood everywhere. *Valenciano*, a Catalan dialect, is gaining ground north of Alicante. You'll also hear A*licantino* and *lemosín*. South of Alicante, *murciano* and its dialects are spoken.

English, French and German are often spoken in the tourist centres.

	Valenciano	Castilian
Good morning	*Bon dia*	*Buenos dias*
Good afternoon/ Good evening	*Bona vesprada*	*Buenas tardes*
Good night	*Bona nit*	*Buenas noches*
Please	*Per favor*	*Por favor*
Thank you	*Gracies*	*Gracias*
You're welcome	*De res*	*De nada*
Good-bye	*Adéu*	*Adiós*

The Berlitz SPANISH PHRASE BOOK AND DICTIONARY covers most situations you are likely to encounter during your travels in Spain. The Berlitz SPANISH-ENGLISH/ENGLISH-SPANISH POCKET DICTIONARY contains 12,500 concepts, plus a menu-reader supplement.

Do you speak English?	**¿Habla usted inglés?**
116 I don't speak Spanish.	**No hablo español.**

LAUNDRY and DRY-CLEANING. Most hotels will handle laundry and dry-cleaning, but they'll usually charge more than a laundry *(lavanderia)* or a dry-cleaners *(tintoreria)*. You'll find do-it-yourself launderettes *(launderama)* only in Benidorm.

When will it be ready	**¿Quando estará listo?**
I must have this for tomorrow morning.	**Lo necesita para mañana.**

LOST PROPERTY. The first thing to do when you discover you've lost something is obviously to retrace your steps. If nothing comes to light, report the loss to the Municipal Police or the Guardia Civil.

I've lost my wallet/handbag/ passport.	**He perdido mi cartera/bolso/ pasaporte.**

MAPS. Road maps are on sale at most petrol stations, bookshops and news-stands. Road and street signs carry place names both in Castilian and *Valenciano*—a fact not reflected on every map. The most detailed—but not *always* foolproof—cartographic information is contained in the official atlas of Spain (scale 1:400,000), issued by the Ministry of Public Works.

The maps in this guide were prepared by Falk-Verlag, Hamburg, who also publish a road map of Spain and Portugal.

a street plan of …	**un plano de la ciudad de …**
a road map of this region	**un mapa de carreteras de esta comarca**

MEDICAL CARE. By far the best solution, to be completely at ease, is to take out a special health insurance policy to cover the risk of illness and accident while on holiday. Your travel agent can also fix you up with Spanish tourist insurance (ASTES), but it is a slow-moving process. ASTES covers doctors' fees and clinical care.

Health care in the resort areas and in the major cities is good but expensive, hence the need for adequate insurance. However, British visitors can qualify for medical care on the Spanish national health service (get a Form E 111 before leaving the U.K.). For minor ailments, visit the local first-aid

M post *(casa de socorro* or *dispensario)*. Away from your hotel, don't hesitate to ask the police or a tourist information office for help.

Pharmacies *(farmacia)* are usually open during normal shopping hours. After hours, at least one per town remains open all night, the *farmacia de guardia*. Its location is posted in the window of all other *farmacias*.

I need a doctor/dentist.	**Necesito un médico/dentista.**
I've a pain here.	**Me duele aquí.**
a fever/sunburn	**fiebre/quemadura del sol**
an upset stomach	**molestias de estómago**

MEETING PEOPLE. Politeness and simple courtesies still matter in Spain. A handshake on greeting and leaving is normal. Always begin any conversation with a *buenos días* (good morning) or *buenas tardes* (good afternoon). Always say *adiós* (good-bye) or, at night, *buenas noches* when leaving. *Por favor* (please) should begin all requests.

The Spanish have their own pace. Not only is it bad manners to try to rush them, but unproductive as well.

MONEY MATTERS

Currency: The monetary unit of Spain is the *peseta* (abbreviated *pta.)*
   Coins: 1, 5, 10, 25, 50, 100, 200 and 500 pesetas.
   Banknotes: 1,000, 2,000, 5,000 and 10,000 pesetas.
   A 5-peseta coin is traditionally called a *duro*, so if someone should quote a price as 10 duros, he means 50 pesetas. For currency restrictions, see ENTRY AND CUSTOMS FORMALITIES

Banking hours: 9 a.m. to 2 p.m., Saturdays to 1 p.m. Outside these hours, currency can usually be changed at a cambio or in your hotel. Always take your passport, as it's the only accepted form of identification.

Credit cards: All the internationally recognized cards are accepted by hotels, restaurants and businesses in Spain.

Eurocheques: You'll have no problem settling bills or paying for purchases with Eurocheques.

Traveller's cheques: In tourist areas, shops and all banks, hotels and travel
118 agencies accept them, though you're likely to get a better exchange rate at a

national or regional bank. Always remember to take your passport with
you if you expect to cash a traveller's cheque.

I want to change some pounds/ dollars.	**Quiero cambiar libras/ dólares.**
Do you accept traveller's cheques?	**¿Acepta usted cheques de viaje?**
Can I pay with this credit card?	**¿Puedo pagar con esta tarjeta de crédito?**

MOSQUITOES. There are rarely more than a few mosquitoes at a given time, but they survive the year round, and just one can ruin a night's sleep. Few hotels, flats or villas have mosquito-proofed windows. Bring or buy your own anti-mosquito devices, whether nets, buzzers, lotions, sprays or incense-type coils that burn all night.

NEWSPAPERS and MAGAZINES *(periódico; revista)*. In tourist towns you can buy most European and British newspapers on the day of publication, including the *International Herald Tribune*. Most glossy European and American magazines are available. The *Costa Blanca News* goes on sale on Fridays and there is a free newspaper, the *Entertainer*.

Have you any English-language newspapers/magazines?	**¿Tienen periódicos/revistas en inglés?**

PHOTOGRAPHY. There's tremendous scope for the keen photographer, but beware of the strong light. For good results don't shoot between 11 a.m. and 3 p.m. unless there's light cloud to soften the sun.

All popular brands and most sizes of film (except 220) are available. Imported films and chemicals are expensive. Spanish-made film is much less expensive and of a reasonable quality.

Shops in major resorts usually provide a reasonably priced 48- or 72-hour processing service for both black-and-white and colour. It's often safer to develop them at home. If possible always keep film—exposed and unexposed—in a refrigerator.

P I'd like a film for this camera.

Quisiera un carrete para esta máquina.

a black-and-white film
un carrete en blanco y negro

a colour-slide film
un carrete de diapositivas

a film for colour pictures
un carrete para película en color

35-mm film
un carrete treinta y cinco

How long will it take to develop (and print) this film?
¿Cuánto tardará en revelar (y sacar copias de) este carrete?

POLICE *(policía)*. There are three police forces in Spain: the *Policía Municipal*, local units who wear a blue uniform; the *Cuerpo Nacional de Policía*, a national anti-crime unit who also wear a blue uniform; and the *Guardia Civil*, the national police force which operates as a highway patrol, who wear a green uniform. Call on any of the three in an emergency.

Where's the nearest police station?
¿Dónde está la comisaría más cercana?

PUBLIC HOLIDAYS *(fiesta)*

January 1	*Año Nuevo*	New Year's Day
January 6	*Epifanía*	Epiphany
May 1	*Día del Trabajo*	Labour Day
July 25	*Santiago Apóstol*	St. James' Day
August 15	*Asunción*	Assumption
October 12	*Fiesta Nacional*	National Holiday (Columbus Day)
November 1	*Todos los Santos*	All Saints' Day
December 6	*Día de la Constitución Española*	Constitution Day
December 25	*Navidad*	Christmas Day
Movable dates:	*Jueves Santo*	Maundy Thursday
	Viernes Santo	Good Friday
	Lunes de Pascua	Easter Monday (Catalonia only)
	Corpus Christi	Corpus Christi
	Inmaculada Concepción	Immaculate Conception (normally December 8)

These are only the national holidays of Spain. October 9th is a local holiday, *Dia de la comunidad valenciana*.

Are you open tomorrow? **¿Está abierto mañana?**

RADIO and TV *(radio; televisión)*. A short-wave set of reasonable quality will pick up all European capitals. Reception of Britain's BBC World Service is usually poor and often unobtainable along the coast. In the winter a good set will pull in the BBC medium and long wave "Home" programmes. The Voice of America usually comes through loud and clear, though in Spain the programme is not received 24 hours a day. The Spanish music programme, *segundo programa*, jazz to Bach but mostly classical, is excellent. It's FM only, around 88 UKW on the band.

Most hotels and bars have television, usually tuned in to sports – including soccer and rugby – bull fighting, variety or nature programmes.

RELIGIOUS SERVICES. The national religion is Roman Catholicism, but other denominations and faiths are represented. Since 1977 the Costa Blanca has had a permanent English-speaking Protestant chaplain. He functions in various churches and centres, mostly between Benidorm and Denia. The Evangelical Church also has a small but strong following; services, in Spanish, are held regularly. The Synagogue in Benidorm (parque Loix) holds Sabbath services on Friday at 20.30. The *Costa Blanca News* carries details of religious services.

SIESTA. A late lunch is often followed by a nap throughout the area, usually between 1 and 5 p.m. Shops re-open at 4 or 5 p.m. until 8 or 9 p.m.

TIME DIFFERENCES. Spanish time coincides with most of Western Europe—Greenwich Mean Time plus one hour. In summer, another hour is added for Daylight Saving Time (Summer Time).

Summer Time chart:

New York	London	**Spain**	Jo'burg	Sydney	Auckland
6 a.m.	11 a.m.	**noon**	noon	8 p.m.	10 p.m.

What time is it? **¿Qué hora es?**

T **TIPPING.** Since a service charge is normally included in hotel and restaurant bills, tipping is not obligatory. However, it's appropriate to tip bellboys, filling-station attendants (for extra services), bullfight ushers, etc. The chart below gives some suggestions as to what to leave.

Hotel porter, per bag	50 ptas.
Maid, for extra services	100–200 ptas.
Lavatory attendant	25–50 ptas.
Waiter	5–10% (optional)
Taxi driver	10%
Hairdresser/Barber	10%
Tourist guide	10%

TOILETS. There are many expressions for "toilets" in Spanish: *aseos, servicios, W.C., water and retretes*. The first terms are the more common.

Where are the toilets? **¿Dónde están los servicios?**

TOURIST INFORMATION OFFICES (*oficinas de turismo*). Spanish National Tourist Offices are maintained throughout the world:

Australia: Level 2-203 Castlereagh Street, NSW, 2000 Sydney South; tel. (2) 264-7966.

Canada: 102 Bloor St. West, 14th Floor, Toronto, Ont. M5S–1M8; tel. (416) 961-3131.

United Kingdom: 57-58, St. James's St., London SW1A 1LD tel. (0171) 499-0901.

USA: Suite 915 East 845, N. Michigan Ave., Chicago, IL 60601; tel. (312) 642-1992.

8383 Wilshire Blvd., Suite 960, Beverly Hills, CA 90211; tel. (213) 658-7188/93.

665 5th Ave., New York, NY 10022; tel. (212) 759-8822.

1221 Brickell Avenue, Miami, FL 33131; tel. (305) 358 1992.

These offices will supply you with a wide range of colourful and informative brochures and maps in English on the various towns and regions in

Spain. They will also let you consult a copy of the master directory of hotels in Spain, listing all facilities and prices.

All major cities and leading resorts in Spain have their own extremely helpful tourist information offices, all of which will be delighted to provide information and brochures on local tourist attractions.

TRANSPORT

Buses: There are good bus services from the Alicante terminal to most towns in the province and further afield, usually every hour. Book your ticket—it will have a numbered seat—from the relevant kiosk inside the hall. The various companies almost always put on sufficient buses to take waiting passengers, so make sure you get the right one; i.e., don't get on the first bus if your ticket says "Autobús 2". If you've got a ticket you've got a bus.

Outside Alicante enquire about bus routes and times at the local tourist office, travel agency or hotel or, in some towns, at the bus terminal, *estación central de autobuses*. Most coastal routes are hourly and reasonably regular. Don't worry unduly if the first bus shoots past full up; there will almost certainly be back-up buses behind. Most towns have their own internal services, usually small buses that buzz from beach to beach. Start looking for the last bus about 8 p.m. Buses are more expensive than the narrow-gauge railway, but less expensive than main line trains.

Taxis*: Spain's taxis compare very favourably to those in the rest of Europe. Wherever you're going, with or without a meter, check the approximate fare *before* setting off. If you travel outside a town, you'll be charged the two-way trip unless there's a return fare. Except in Benidorm and Alicante, taxis tend to disappear around midnight, earlier out of season. Arrange to be fetched or you may find yourself stranded.

By Spanish law taxis may only take four persons per vehicle (although some are willing to risk a fifth if it is a baby or child).

A green light and/or a *Libre* ("free") sign indicates a taxi is available.

Trains *(tren)*: A narrow-gauge line runs from Alicante to Denia, taking about 2 hours 15 minutes, as the train makes frequent stops. From Alicante, main line trains reach to most corners of Spain. Local trains are slow, stopping at most stations. Long-distance services are fast and punctu- **123**

T al. First-class coaches are comfortable; second-class, adequate. Tickets can be purchased at travel agencies as well as at the stations *(estación de ferro-carril)*. For long trips, seat reservations are advisable on most Spanish trains.

Talgo, Intercity, Electrotren, Ter, Tren Estrella	Luxury diesel, first and second classes; supplementary charge over regular fare
Expreso, Rápido	Long-distance expresses, stopping at main stations only; supplementary charge
Omnibus, Tranvía, Automotor	Local trains, with frequent stops, usually second class only
Auto Expreso	Car train
coche cama	Sleeping-car with 1-, 2- or 3-bed compartments, washing facilities
coche comedor	Dining-car
litera	Sleeping-berth car *(couchette)* with blankets, sheets and pillows
furgón de equipajes	Luggage van (baggage car); only registered luggage permitted

When's the next bus to …?	**¿Cuándo sale el próximo autobús para …?**
single (one-way)	**ida**
return (round-trip)	**ida y vuelta**
When/Which is the best train to …?	**¿Cuándo/Cuál es el mejor tren para …?**
I'd like to make seat reservations.	**Quiero reservar asientos.**

W WATER *(agua)*. The rain in Spain doesn't fall much along the Costa Blanca, where tap water is a precious commodity. There are periodic shortages, causing problems that can prove a nuisance factor (water turned off at night, etc.).

When Spaniards drink water, it is almost invariably bottled water, not tap water. It is quite common to order water sent to one's room. If you're particularly sensitive to water, watch out, too, for the ice cubes in drinks.

a bottle of mineral water	**una botella de agua mineral**
fizzy (carbonated)/still	**con/sin gas**
Is this drinking water?	**¿El agua es potable?**

SOME USEFUL EXPRESSIONS

yes/no	**sí/no**
please/thank you	**por favor/gracias**
excuse me/you're welcome	**perdone/de nada**
where/when/how	**dónde/cuándo/cómo**
how long/how far	**cuánto tiempo/a qué distancia**
yesterday/today/tomorrow	**ayer/hoy/mañana**
day/week/month/year	**día/semana/mes/año**
left/right	**izquierda/derecha**
up/down	**arriba/abajo**
good/bad	**bueno/malo**
big/small	**grande/pequeño**
cheap/expensive	**barato/caro**
hot/cold	**caliente/frío**
old/new	**viejo/nuevo**
open/closed	**abierto/cerrado**
Waiter!/Waitress!	**¡Camarero!/¡Camarera!**
I'd like…	**Quisiera…**
How much is that?	**¿Cuánto es?**
What time is it?	**¿Qué hora es?**
What does this mean?	**¿Qué quiere decir esto?**
Is there anyone here who speaks English?	**¿Hay alguien aquí que hable inglés?**
I don't understand.	**No comprendo.**

Index

An asterisk (*) next to a page number indicates a map reference.